I0818126

Switzerland.

A land of snow-capped peaks, clockwork precision and powdery slopes. But look closer and you'll find more than what's on posters and postcards. The country thrives in the balance between hushed tradition and loud reinvention, where avant-garde galleries hide in medieval alleyways and defiant graffiti shadows iconic design. Switzerland will exceed your expectations, but only if you dare to expect more.

LOST iN takes you inside the modern Swiss pulse. You'll discover high-altitude creatives and urban alchemists, vinyl bars and floating hot tubs, fearless architects and lakeside vineyards, the thunderous spray of Europe's biggest waterfall. You'll even stand on the ledge where Sherlock Holmes met his dramatic end. Along the way, you'll meet the mountain guide chasing impossible lines on vertical slopes, the indie designer dismantling the home aesthetic, one of the youngest chefs ever to command three Michelin stars, and the photographer documenting underground youth culture across generations.

From the eerie stillness of forgotten passes to the rattle of spray cans claiming city walls, Switzerland refuses to be boxed in. Experience it like an insider, an explorer, a rebel. Get lost in the Switzerland that breaks its own rules.

Interviews

Features

Photo: Patrick Robert Doyle

Set high above Grindelwald, Lake Bachalpsee mirrors the sky with near-perfect stillness, its twin basins reflecting the icy spires of the Bernese giants. The high-elevation lake is known as the "Blue Jewel" of the Swiss Alps, while nearby Schreckhorn has the less inviting nickname, "Peak of Terror," for its soaring height and sharp granite ridges. At sunrise, alpenglow ignites the mountain's ridges as the lake turns to liquid gold. Despite Bachalpsee's accessibility, the atmosphere feels remote, an almost otherworldly place where the wind sweeps across stone and the scale of the Alps overwhelms.

• Lake Bachalpsee, Grindelwald

Photo: Willian Justen

Top Five

Landmarks, legends and local secrets—where the Switzerland you came for meets the one you didn't expect.

Skate Spots

- ☐ Port Land Bowl, Basel
- ☐ Betongarta Obere Au, Chur
- ☐ Skatepark de Plainpalais, Geneva
- ☐ Freestyle Academy, Laax
- ☐ Bäckeranlage, Zurich

Alpine Swims

- ☐ Aare River, Bern
- ☐ Caumasee, Flims
- ☐ Bains des Pâquis, Geneva
- ☐ Lido Riva Caccia, Lugano
- ☐ Seebad Enge, Zurich

Street Art All-Stars

- ☐ Harald Naegeli
- ☐ Nevercrew
- ☐ One Truth Bros
- ☐ Saype
- ☐ REDL

Born in Switzerland

- ☐ Mary Shelley's *Frankenstein*
- ☐ Einstein's Theory of Relativity
- ☐ The first LSD trip
- ☐ The World Wide Web (WWW)
- ☐ Helvetica typeface

Gallery Circuit

- ☐ Starkart Urban Art Gallery, Zurich
- ☐ Artstübli, Basel
- ☐ Galerie Soon, Zurich
- ☐ Kolly Gallery, Zurich
- ☐ Guillaume Daeppen, Basel

Photo: Patrick Robert Doyle

Ethnic Eats

- ☐ Peruvian: Nido, Zurich
- ☐ Chinese: Golden Dragon, Davos
- ☐ Lebanese: Arabesque, Geneva
- ☐ Japanese: Megu, Gstaad
- ☐ Tibetan: Tibetasia, Zurich

Tourist Blind Spots

- ☐ Creux du Van
- ☐ Greina Plateau
- ☐ Val Bavona
- ☐ Schöllenen Gorge
- ☐ Lower Engadin

Sustainability Now

- ☐ Climeworks
- ☐ Villars Institute
- ☐ GreenUp
- ☐ Holcim Foundation
- ☐ Swisstainable

Village Charm

- ☐ Morcote
- ☐ Stein am Rhein
- ☐ Gruyères
- ☐ Appenzell
- ☐ Soglio

Artist Residencies

- ☐ Fondation Jan Michalski
- ☐ Villa Ruffieux
- ☐ Arts at CERN
- ☐ La Becque
- ☐ Fundaziun Nairs

The Swiss Circuit

A Geography of Moments

The Grand Tour of Switzerland rewrites the rules of the classic road trip. It is a constantly shifting panorama where glacier-fed lakes give way to hushed alpine villages, and daring modern architecture anchors centuries-old cities. Hit the road and surrender to the route.

Between April and October, Switzerland shows its friendliest side: high-altitude passes cleared of winter snow, evenings that linger into twilight and clear views of distant glaciers. This is no highway commute. It is a 1,021-mile journey across eight stages, carved almost entirely into the backroads. More than 650 signs and a dedicated navigation app help point the way, steering you away from the tourist crowds and deep into the country's hidden pockets. The route features 22 lakes, 13 UNESCO World Heritage Sites, five Alpine passes, two biosphere reserves and four distinct languages. Yet out on the asphalt, these statistics dissolve into encounters, experiences and memories that stick with you long after the adventure ends.

Photo: Robert Pügner

The Grand Tour of Switzerland is less a single path and more a curated gallery. In Zurich, the twin-towered Grossmünster dominates the skyline, while Stein am Rhein offers a painted history where medieval façades are punctuated by ornate bay windows. The perspective widens in the Engadin, where the broad sweep of Muottas Muragl overlooks the peaks, and shifts again in Bern's Old Town with sandstone arcades that stretch for miles beneath the city's medieval rooflines.

This is a corridor through time, cutting through the echoes of the Ice Age and the imprints of Roman legionnaires. In the Jura mountains, the watchmaking streets of La Chaux-de-Fonds and Le Locle reveal a legacy of mechanical precision, while the lush marshes of the Entlebuch biosphere offer a serene, wild contrast. No journey is complete without the Swiss Alps Jungfrau–Aletsch. From the Moosfluh, Bettmerhorn or Eggishorn viewpoints, the 14-mile-long Aletsch Glacier stretches to the horizon.

The heritage of the land is visible everywhere, from the sweeping curves of the Tremola to the pristine wilderness of the Swiss National Park. Even the earth itself tells a story at the Sardona Tectonic Arena, where dramatic geology showcases a landscape shaped over millennia. Along the shores of Lake Lucerne, the chime of the carillon at the Tell Chapel (of William Tell fame) echoes across water that has carried myth and history in equal measure.

The E-Grand Tour of Switzerland also points toward the future as the world's first fully electric road trip, supported by a dense network of charging stations. The route is yours to curate, so set your priorities. Foodies can head to markets, wineries and cheese dairies like the *Emmental Show Dairy* in Affoltern im Emmental. Architectural enthusiasts, meanwhile, can explore historic bridges, thermal bathhouses and icons of modernism such as the Goetheanum in Dornach, with its sculpted concrete curves challenging the very definition of structure.

The journey is punctuated by moments that demand a picnic stop, perhaps in the sunny vineyards of Riex where the vines cascade toward the shores of Lake Geneva. To fuel these detours, around 50 local outposts offer the Grand Tour Snack Box, a reusable container for two that you can replenish with regional specialties. For those chasing the perfect frame, a series of 92 marked photo spots act as your scout. The locations are chosen for their exceptional views, composition and light, ensuring the perspective is always just right. Yet these points are less about trophy hunting and more about anchoring the moment.

The route provides the framework, but the detours, spontaneous breaks and chance encounters are what define the soul of the map. All information, along with a free app, is available online from Switzerland Tourism. To truly absorb the Grand Tour of Switzerland, we recommend carving out 7 to 14 days, though the itinerary is yours to dismantle and rebuild as you see fit.

The road is ready. All that's left is for you to choose a direction.

• **Grand Tour of Switzerland, switzerland.com/grandtour**

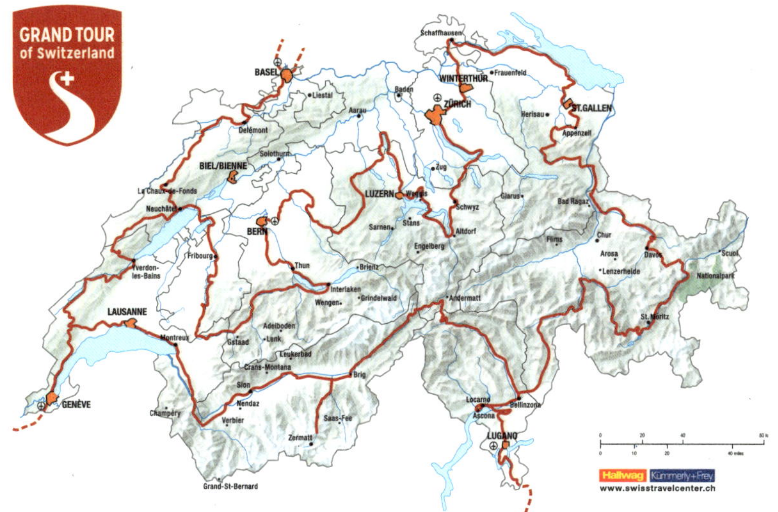

Explore

Streets, Shores and Summits

Forget the idea of an off-season. In Switzerland, the momentum doesn't stop, it simply shifts gears.

One moment, you're slipping into the turquoise chill of Lake Brienz, the summer sun radiating off the limestone peaks above. The next, you're breathing in the mountain air of a Zermatt morning, the soft sink of fresh powder under your boots. The scene shifts, and you discover street art in the high mountains, fine dining in a castle and hot tubs floating in a lake. You might leave a wintry après-ski in St. Moritz only to return months later and find those same slopes drowned in a sea of summer green.

Your journey across the Swiss grid is measured in more than just distance and altitude. It's about transitioning between moods, micro-climates and different ways of living, like navigating a series of distinct worlds, each with its own gravity.

We've mapped the essential destinations for those ready to explore. We start where the pulse is loudest: Zurich.

Photo: Andreas Gucklhorn

Zurich

Liquid Days, Neon Nights

Zurich deserves more time than just a layover between the airport and the Alps. This is a city where locals swim in the river at lunch, dine at Michelin Green Star restaurants and dance the weekend away without curfew. From the central Bahnhofstrasse, the city's neighborhoods stretch out in every direction.

As the Bahnhofstrasse leads you from the train station to Lake Zurich, leave behind the designer stores and step into the city's local rhythm. Paths trace the lake banks for strolls and runs, or you can simply sit and enjoy the views with a takeaway lunch. Westward, the neighborhood of Enge's lakeside Badi (public bath) is open year-round, offering summer swimming and winter saunas with cold lake plunges. For those who prefer indoor wellness experiences, the Roman-Irish baths of the *Hürlimann & Spa* flow from room to room under the original arches of an old brewery. The spa's rooftop pool, warm enough for all seasons, has an epic view across the city.

Leaving the lake behind, follow the streets into *Wiedikon*, where young chefs challenge the idea that Swiss food is just cheese, potatoes and chocolate. This area is where chefs can experiment, mixing immigrant culture with Swiss precision. One example is Chef Zineb "Zizi" Hattab, who emerged from the kitchen of three-Michelin-star chef Andreas Caminada. Zizi's vegan empire, including *Kle*, helped kickstart Zurich's Michelin Green Star movement. Zurich is now a leading European city for sustainable gastronomy, ahead of the movement's philosophical heart, Copenhagen.

Zurich West is where the city is at its most unguarded. The neighborhood built its identity around repurposed industrial buildings, a creative past still visible alongside the city's tallest building, Prime Tower. *Frau Gerolds Garten* embodies this perfectly: a seasonal gathering place where locals come to eat fondue by the fire in winter and dance under open skies when the sun shines. Artisanal markets fill the gaps between seasons. Cult *Gelateria di Berna* rewards the inevitable queue with what locals consider to be the city's best ice cream.

Across the green stretch of Josefwiese park, an arcade of independent shops and restaurants lines the arches of the city's longest railway viaduct.

Closer to Zurich's main station, Langstrasse is the city's most contradictory neighborhood. Natural wine bars like *Gamper* and destination restaurants such as *Gül* sit streets away from the red-light district and clubs that keep going long after everywhere else has closed.

After midnight, Zurich reveals its other reputation: the highest density of nightlife in Switzerland. Party 'til dawn from Langstrasse to the gritty venues of Zurich West, or on to the more glamorous *AURA* and *Jade*. Kaufleuten has anchored the city's night scene for generations and once hosted figures from the Dada art movement, a good reminder that Zurich's cultural life has always run deep.

Being one of the most expensive cities in the world doesn't mean everything requires a banker's budget. *Kunsthaus*, Switzerland's largest art museum and home to an extensive Dada collection and works by Swiss artist Alberto Giacometti, opens free on Wednesdays. The *Swiss National Museum*'s permanent collection "Simply Zurich" is free every day. At *ETH Zurich*, Einstein's alma mater, free tours include a visit to the Nobel Prize winner's former locker.

Escaping the trams and foot traffic of Switzerland's largest city is as easy as heading uphill. Flanked by Uetliberg to the west and Zürichberg to the east, the forest is never far. On weekends, locals take the Dolderbahn up to the Dolder Grand and hike deep into the forest, stopping at *Wirtschaft Degenried* for brunch or lunch. Detour to the Lorenkopf and climb the 150 steps for a view back over the city and the Alps beyond. In winter, the same Dolderbahn brings locals back up to one of Europe's largest artificial rinks.

Come December, the city glows. Lucy, named after the Beatles song, leads a path of light along the Bahnhofstrasse from the train station to the lake. Locals gather at Christmas market stalls for lunch or after-work Glühwein, while choirs perform nightly on a stage shaped like a giant Christmas tree. The Illuminarium light festival brings the Swiss National Museum's façade to life after dark. Meanwhile, hundreds of swimmers dressed as Samichlaus (Santa Claus) plunge into the cold waters of the Limmat. In summer, the river becomes the beating heart of the city. Locals swim at lunch, float downstream and dry off on the wooden decks of the Flussbäder (river baths). The Limmat threads through it all.

St. Moritz

Between Sun and Snow

The true allure of St. Moritz isn't a single bar, hotel or boutique. It's that this village in Switzerland's southeastern corner basks in a legendary 300 days of sunshine, a golden light that bounces off Lake St. Moritz with grand dame hotels sitting proudly above its shores.

On the opposite bank, even the youth hostel wakes up to the same vintage light. The mountain peaks catch the sun while larch forests—green in summer, bare in winter and gorgeously golden in autumn—are the lungs of the Engadin.

"The air is a diamond," Friedrich Nietzsche once wrote of the local area, "the most wonderful thing I have ever known." And it's easy to see what he means: hiking boots crunching along gravel paths, streams weaving through lush green meadows. Nature is as idyllic as it gets here, with fingernail-size wild strawberries ready to pick as you walk.

All hiking paths lead somewhere spectacular, like Alp Laret, reached on foot in about an hour or by the Celerina cable car in 30 minutes. Order *Kaiserschmarrn,* pillow-like pancakes, with fresh ricotta made from the cows grazing outside. Looking up from the plate, you'll find alpine peaks in every direction.

When the trails lead downhill, the lakes take over. Walk past the lake into the larch forest, which opens up onto Lej da Staz. A wooden jetty leads out into an alpine painting, the backdrop to July's Festival da Jazz. Come autumn, Lej da Staz becomes a pilgrimage for Swiss locals. When the larch needles turn, the lake's reflection shifts from royal blue to gold, settling the valley into calm before the business of winter begins. Further afield, both the Morteratsch Glacier and Alp Grüm are easily reached by train along the Bernina route and compete for the best fall scenery.

When winter arrives, so do the skiers, both alpine and cross-country. The crowds build from the moment the slopes open in late fall, peaking at Christmas and again during Europe's ski holidays in February. Those in the know wait until the crowds pass. By March, the slopes are quieter, it's terrace weather, and ski jackets remain unzipped.

When the mountains release you, the village draws you in. Head to *Café Belmont*, where German, Italian, English and Romansh, Switzerland's fourth official language, drift between tables. Where else would you find a curated champagne list and hiking boots at the same table? From croissants to charcuterie, the menu draws traffic all day long. For something stronger, *N/5 THE Bar* at *Grace La Margna* keeps pouring even when other five-star establishments have closed for the shoulder season. Or simply fill a water bottle from one of St. Moritz's fountains: the grand cru of tap water.

On sunny days, grab a Kalbsbratwurst from *Hanselmann*'s kiosk in the center of town. For truffled pizza, *Chesa Veglia*'s pizzeria sits in a house that dates back to 1658, making it the oldest in St. Moritz. Some of the best chefs in the world call St. Moritz home at one time or another, among them *La Coupole - Matsuhisa*, a restaurant inside Europe's first indoor tennis hall.

Chefs and concepts come and go with the seasons, but what starts as a pop-up sometimes sticks around, like *Super Mountain Market*, a concept store and community hub bringing together local artisans and gastronomes.

From Nietzsche to painter Giovanni Segantini, creatives have been drawn to the Engadin valley for generations. The *Berry Museum* showcases local artist Peter Robert Berry II (1864–1942), known as the Van Gogh of the Alps. The *Segantini Museum*, built from the artist's own sketch, houses his *Alpine Triptych: Life, Nature and Death* under its dome. More contemporary work can be found at *Galerie von Opel*. Deep in the forest, the *Mili Weber Museum* is a house preserved exactly as the artist left it, a fairy-tale world of her paintings and the craftsmanship of her architect brother Emil. Tours by appointment only.

But the museums are no competition for what's outside. It always comes back to the landscape. The air is sharp, the light shimmers as the sun sets behind the mountains, and the village hums. You don't need to reach deep into your pockets to experience why people return year after year. That diamond air is free. So is the yearning to return.

Photo: Oskar Gross

Zermatt

Where the Matterhorn Meets Italy

There are mountains, and then there is the Matterhorn. The world's most photographed peak rises above Zermatt, a legendary mountaineering base and ski resort in the Swiss Alps, with sculptural precision, magnetic in every season. Yet to focus on the icon alone is to miss the scale of the landscape around it. Zermatt sits in a high-alpine amphitheater surrounded by 38 peaks more than 14,000 feet tall, braided with glaciers and laced with trails. It feels vast and elemental, as epic as the peak that towers above it.

Summer here is an antidote to Mediterranean heat. While cities shimmer, Zermatt offers clear air, cool mornings and long, sunlit afternoons. Hikers set out early on trails that wind past larch forests and alpine meadows. One of the most rewarding walks begins at Rotenboden and leads down to Riffelsee, a small lake that on still days perfectly reflects the Matterhorn. Valais Blacknose sheep graze nearby between June and September, their spiral horns and dark faces giving them a storybook charm. At Gornergrat, you can meet the GPS-tracked sheep and talk to the guide, who knows each animal by name.

For a deeper immersion, follow the Matterhorn Glacier Trail from Trockener Steg to Schwarzsee. The path runs beneath the mountain's towering faces, close enough to study its strata and feel its presence without the rope and crampons required for the summit. For a classic alpine walk, the 5-Lakes Hike above Zermatt strings together a series of crystal-clear mountain lakes, most of which act as mirrors for the Matterhorn when the waters are calm. The trail is well-marked and surprisingly accessible, but the views feel anything but ordinary.

Crossing the border to Italy is another adventure. The Matterhorn Alpine Crossing carries visitors by gondola over high ice and rock to Cervinia in Italy, passing above the Theodul Glacier. For centuries, the nearby Theodul Pass marked an important trade route between Switzerland and Italy, linking the valleys on either side of the Alps.

In less than an hour and a half, the language, pace and cuisine shift. Espresso replaces café crème, pasta takes center stage and tiramisu is non-negotiable. The change feels surprisingly immediate. Two cultures, just a ridge of snow apart, and a reminder that Zermatt has always looked both north and south.

Back in the village, Bahnhofstrasse (Zermatt's main thoroughfare) hums gently with life. In summer, 60 to 70 Valais Blackneck goats parade through the street twice a day, bells clanging as they head to pasture. It is a cherished tradition, but also a rather bucolic spectacle if you're in town. Locals greet one another in the thick Valais dialect, a musical German that can puzzle visitors from other parts of Switzerland. Conversations drift between mountaineering plans, weather forecasts and where to find the best lunch with a view.

As for the latter, Zermatt's culinary scene consistently surprises first-time guests. For a long lunch overlooking the Matterhorn, *Alphitta* at Riffelalp pairs mountain classics with a front-row panorama. On Gornergrat at *3100 Kulmhotel* (the highest hotel in the Swiss Alps), *SayCheese* celebrates Swiss cheese culture at 10,000 feet, while the restaurant at *Matterhorn Glacier Paradise* serves dishes and a view in one of the highest dining rooms in Europe. There's more. Down at Furi, a family-friendly hamlet south of Zermatt, *MARMO* interprets alpine cuisine with a modern touch. In the village, *Brasserie Uno* holds a Michelin Green Star, reflecting Zermatt's commitment to sustainability alongside quality.

That commitment runs deeper than the plate. The Gornergrat Railway generates electricity as its trains descend, feeding energy back into the system for future journeys. The Zermatt Bergbahnen is TourCert certified and invests in solar panels, annual Clean Up Days and ongoing environmental initiatives, underscoring a long-term vision for responsible tourism. In Zermatt, sustainability is not a slogan but a practical necessity in a fragile alpine environment.

Winter brings a different rhythm. Skiers trace lines beneath the Matterhorn, while others ascend to Gornergrat for sunrise, watching alpenglow ignite a ring of 14,000-foot peaks. As night falls, special dining experiences under the stars transform the mountains into candlelit stages. Snow softens the landscape, but the village remains lively, fueled by good food and the warmth of a community that lives with altitude year-round.

Ask a local how they spend a Sunday, and the answer is simple: outside. Hiking, skiing, climbing or just walking high above the rooftops. The mountains are not a backdrop here, they're a playground on the doorstep. That, along with the village's personal feel, might be Zermatt's biggest draw. Talk to a mountain guide about changing conditions, a chef about local produce or a shepherd about his flock. Each conversation sheds light on different layers of mountain living.

The Matterhorn may draw you here. The breadth of experience, from glacier trails and goat parades to towering peaks and sky-high Swiss cheese, will make you stay.

Bern

Switzerland's Laid-Back Capital

Switzerland's capital moves at its own pace. Bern is famous for its relaxed mood—the locals even speak a little slower—and the city's easygoing atmosphere is part of its charm.

The medieval Old Town, a UNESCO World Heritage Site, feels almost untouched by time. Sandstone arcades stretch for miles, historic fountains bubble with drinkable water and everyday life unfolds between markets, cafés and independent shops.

Despite its grand history, Bern never feels like a museum. Beneath the arcades you'll find small boutiques and studios run by local designers rather than big global brands. Weekly markets fill the squares with regional produce, while hidden gems such as *Kunsthalle Bern* keep the city's contemporary art scene lively. For dinner, head to *Restaurant Cima* in the Old Town, where alpine ingredients like grains, mountain herbs and cheeses shape a seasonal menu backed by a wine cellar of more than 500 bottles.

As in the rest of the country, nature is never far away. Bern is often described as an urban nature hub, where green spaces sit right alongside city streets. Just 10 minutes from the center, the Gurten (Bern's local mountain) offers sweeping views over the city and all the way to the snowy Alps. Walking trails, picnic spots and restaurants make it an easy escape year-round.

In summer, the city's relationship with nature becomes even more obvious. Experienced swimmers swap the pavement for the Aare River currents, floating downstream through the city. If you prefer dry land, follow the scenic Green Aare Walk, a riverside path that reveals leafy parks and quiet corners just steps from the Old Town.

When evening arrives, Bern's nightlife buzzes beneath the streets. Many of the city's bars are tucked into vaulted cellars, often pouring local craft beers, fitting for a place known as Switzerland's beer capital thanks to its remarkable number of microbreweries.

With a cloudy pint of Bärner Müntschi in hand and the Aare flowing nearby, the city's slow-burning charm takes over. It's a reminder that in Bern, the best itinerary is the one that allows you to stay a while.

Gstaad

Silent Luxury in the Alps

Tucked into the Bernese Oberland, Gstaad has long cultivated a reputation for what locals call "silent luxury."

There are no flashing signs or towering hotel blocks here. Instead, wooden chalets line the promenade, flower boxes spill over balconies and cowbells echo across meadows. With roughly the same number of residents as there are cows, Gstaad keeps its scale deliberately human and deeply alpine.

Strict building regulations help shape the atmosphere. For decades, new homes have been required to follow the traditional three-story chalet style, creating a village that feels cohesive and nostalgic, even as it quietly attracts royalty, artists and global travelers seeking privacy. Among its most devoted admirers is screen icon Julie Andrews. In the early 1970s, she funded the village's first Christmas lights, paying for their upkeep for more than a decade. Each winter, the chalets still glow with understated sparkle.

"Gstaad is the last paradise in a crazy world," she once said, and on a snowy evening beneath softly lit eaves, it is easy to understand why.

Overlooking it all stands the *Gstaad Palace*, its turrets rising above the rooftops like a storybook castle. From its terrace, the village appears almost cinematic: church spire, chalet roofs and mountain ridgelines layered against the sky.

Despite its polished image, Gstaad is built for the outdoors. In winter, more than 125 miles of slopes stretch across the region, reaching altitudes of 10,000 feet at the Glacier 3000 toboggan run. Wide pistes, glacier runs and panoramic views draw skiers who appreciate space and scenery as much as sport. Summer reveals a different yet equally idyllic vibe, with hiking trails that wind past flowery pastures and dairy farms crafting nutty mountain cheese.

Gstaad's cultural calendar adds another layer. Each July, the EFG Swiss Open Gstaad brings world-class tennis to 3,500 feet, where the thin air increases the ball speed. Often called the Wimbledon of the Alps, the tournament offers 250 ATP points and unfolds against a dramatic mountain backdrop, combining more than a century of history with fresh alpine air.

This is Gstaad in a nutshell: good mountains, good cheese and a little low-key glamour.

Interlaken

Between the Lakes

Sitting in an ancient glacial valley between two lakes, Interlaken is almost unbeatable as a base for exploring the Swiss Alps. From here, meandering roads and historic railways wind across the Bernese Oberland toward the dizzying heights of the nearby summits. The town is perhaps best known as the gateway to the Jungfrau Region and the ski resorts of Mürren, Wengen and Grindelwald, with an open setting that provides enticing views of the snowy peaks beyond.

Interlaken's wide selection of activities, from skiing, snowboarding and sledding to paragliding, swimming and rafting, have earned it the title of year-round adventure capital of Europe. Still, adrenaline junkies coming to this region shouldn't overlook the jumping-off point itself. Explore the compact center, with its traditional Swiss chalets, colorful flower boxes and Belle Époque–style buildings. Walk along the Höheweg Promenade, lined with hotels and manicured gardens, or travel as the locals do and hop on a bike.

In the heart of town, Michelin-starred *Radius* by Stefan Beer works with produce sourced from within 30 miles of the kitchen, including wood sorrel from Uetendorf and mirabelle plums from the hotel garden, while *Spatz Café & Wine Bar* serves coffee, wine and light bites from its perch overlooking the river Aare. The ultimate foodie experience, however, has to be raclette rafting. Starting in Bönigen and ending in Interlaken, the trips are run by professional guides who paddle the rafts along the water as passengers tuck into bubbling hot cheese and boiled spuds.

Interlaken's home mountain is Harder Kulm. A steep hike or a ride in a funicular built in 1908 takes you to the pine-forested peak and the turreted restaurant up top. Stop for platters of air-dried beef, smoked meats and alpine cheese, or one of the several fondues, such as the Vacherin and Gruyère mix, served with potatoes and Grindelwald-made bread. In summer, it's a great spot to watch the sun set over the valley.

On the way up and down, keep an eye out for a man's face in the crags below the summit. Known as the Hardermannli, it's said to be a monk from the Interlaken Monastery who was turned to stone after chasing a girl over the cliff's edge.

To the west of Interlaken is Lake Thun, its deep blue waters surrounded by towering mountains, castles, fortresses and even a few vineyards. On the water, a historic paddle steamer known as the Blümlisalp glides quietly across the surface. Places to stop include the St. Beatus Caves with grottos, chasms and vast halls carved out of the limestone, and charming lakeside towns such as the Mediterranean-like Merligen and romantic Oberhofen. Those in the know head to *Pier 17* for sesame bagels with homemade guacamole or salads loaded with burrata and basil. On the northwestern tip is Thun, where locals gather every Wednesday and Saturday for the market on the river island of Bälliz. And in autumn and winter, an electric sauna boat floats on the lake, with the option to dive off and cool down at any time.

To the east of Interlaken is the smaller Lake Brienz, with an intense turquoise hue created by fine particles of glacial sediment in the water. Boat trips connect sights along the shore, from well-trodden Iseltwald to the Giessbach Falls, which cascades down 14 separate steps. Stop at the fairy-tale-like *Grandhotel Giessbach*, built between 1873 and 1874, for a slice of carrot cake on the spacious terrace and a different view of

Photo: Ollie Craig

the waterfall. Alternatively, you can head out onto the water on guided kayak tours, aboard high-speed jet boats or in a relaxing HotTug, a floating hot tub heated by a small stove.

On the far shore is Brienz, the center of traditional woodcarving in the country. The *School of Woodcarving* has provided training in a variety of wood crafts since 1884 and remains the only institution in Switzerland where young people can professionally learn such skills. There's also a museum dedicated to the history of woodcarving in the area. Not far away are the headquarters of *Trauffer*, the company behind the iconic wooden cows. You can make and paint your own, or head straight to the gift shop for the ultimate Swiss souvenir.

Jungfrau Region

More Than Just Famous Landmarks

A world-renowned destination, the Jungfrau Region likely appears on many bucket lists. Visitors flock here for the mighty Eiger–Mönch–Jungfrau trio and the epic engineering that conquers the dramatic rock faces and lofty peaks. Start with the big guns, but also leave time to discover the local culture, cuisine and villages like Meiringen, Lauterbrunnen, Grindelwald, Wengen and Mürren.

The pioneering Jungfrau Railway opened in 1912, connecting the Kleine Scheidegg pass to the Jungfraujoch at 11,332 feet. The rack railway cuts into the rock of the Eiger and Mönch mountains, passing through deep tunnels on its way up to Europe's highest railway station. The final stop, known as the Top of Europe, has jaw-dropping views of the surrounding peaks and the Aletsch Glacier.

The second crowning achievement in the region is the revolving restaurant at the top of the Schilthorn, *Piz Gloria*, which takes 45 minutes to complete one full rotation. Made famous by the 1969 James Bond film *On Her Majesty's Secret Service*, it is now the place to go for brunch rather than a martini. The new cable car that carries people to the top, the Schilthornbahn 20XX, also has a claim to fame. With a 58-degree gradient, the lower section between the valley and the village of Mürren is the world's steepest aerial cableway.

Perched above the Lauterbrunnen Valley, car-free Mürren trades the rumble of engines for the peaceful silence of a village governed by nature. It is here that the *Hotel Mürren Palace* served as a meeting point for high society in the 20th century and where the first slalom races were held in 1922, organized by British alpinist Arnold Lunn. Gift shops selling chocolate, cowbells and cuckoo-clock magnets fill several of the stone and timber cottages, but *Alti Metzg* remains the go-to address for regional cheese, pasta and meat, the connected bistro using ingredients from the store.

Back at the foot of the Eiger, the village of Grindelwald has had a bit of a glow-up in recent years. A number of new hotels and restaurants have popped up alongside après-ski favorites like the *Avocado Bar* in town and *Bus Stop* bar on the slopes. In the center of Grindelwald, *The Cork Club* showcases Swiss winemakers from the Mémoire des Vins Suisses association, while the restaurant in the Scandi-inspired *Hotel Fiescherblick* recently earned its first Michelin star. The four- to six-course menu focuses on seasonal produce and local heritage with dishes like sourdough with burnt butter, mushroom and sunflower seed pâté, or lingonberries with chestnut and honey. For more alpine artistry, swing by *Eigerness Der Laden*, a shop stocking raw-milk Tomme Fleurette from the Rougemont dairy, craft beer from *3970 Nordwand Bräu* brewery and other regional products.

In Meiringen, it's all about meringues, said to have been first produced in the village in the 17th century. *Frutal Bäckerei*, a confectionery and bakery, makes them daily, along with other sweet treats. Don't miss the whimsical and wacky *Tatzelwurm*, an éclair-based dessert inspired by a mythical, dragon-like creature from the Alps. There are Sherlock Holmes chocolates, too, reflecting a valley-wide nod to the fictional English detective who fell to his death at the nearby Reichenbach Falls.

Back outdoors, winter sports feel effortless, with slopes running straight into some village centers and lifts always within easy reach. You can zoom down the legendary Lauberhorn World Cup course, ski under the lights on the Hasliberg slopes or take on Europe's longest sledding run, Big Pintenfritz.

Then there are the *Velogemel*, traditional wooden snow bikes, that can only be rented in Grindelwald. Deriving their name from the Swiss-German words *Velo* (bicycle) and *Gemel* (sled), these curious contraptions glide smoothly over the frozen ground, but their lack of brakes requires digging your feet firmly into the snow to stop or slow down.

After a few days, you might start to recognize the melodic Bernese Oberland dialect, not dissimilar to the slow rhythm of daily life. Despite its international stardom, the pace in this region is steady and unhurried, and the people have a deeply ingrained respect for nature. Staying on marked paths, closing farm gates and greeting cows or other animals like familiar neighbors are all part of an unwritten code. A common saying in this region is *Obe isch's am schönschte*, meaning "Up here it's most beautiful." It's hard to argue with that.

Geneva

Diplomacy, Watchmaking and Lake Life

Geneva has long balanced international influence with a strong local character.

Diplomats, bankers and watchmakers move through the same streets, while café terraces fill with a mix of languages that reflects the city's global role. As the European base for organizations such as the United Nations and Red Cross, Geneva often feels outward-looking. Yet its daily life remains shaped by the lake and the surrounding mountains.

The most visible landmark is the Jet d'Eau, a plume of water that rises nearly 500 feet above the harbor. What began in the 19th century as part of a hydraulic power system has become Geneva's defining emblem. From the lakeside promenade, a walk along the stone jetty brings you close enough to feel the fine mist drifting across the water when the wind shifts, though hopping on the yellow Mouettes Genevoises shuttle boat offers an even better perspective.

Just uphill from the waterfront lies the Vieille Ville, Geneva's Old Town, where narrow lanes wind between townhouses and quaint squares. At its heart stands *St. Pierre Cathedral*, a building whose foundations date to the 12th century and which later became closely linked to the Protestant Reformation through John Calvin. Climbing the tower reveals sweeping views over terra-cotta rooftops, the lake and the distant Alps.

A short distance north, broad parkland surrounds the *Palais des Nations*, built in the 1930s as the headquarters of the League of Nations and now home to the United Nations Office at Geneva. Guided visits pass through assembly halls and council chambers where international negotiations continue today.

The city's reputation for precision also has deep roots in watchmaking. The *Patek Philippe Museum* in the Plainpalais district traces five centuries of horology through historic watches, enamel miniatures and intricate automata.

Despite its global reputation, much of Geneva's appeal lies in simple rituals around the lake. Locals gather at Bains des Pâquis to swim and sunbathe, while historic paddle steamers cross the water toward nearby towns. As evening falls, the quays fill with walkers and cyclists and the light softens across the Jura, the mountain range forming a natural border between Switzerland and France. On clear days Mont Blanc appears on the horizon, a reminder that even in this international city, the surrounding landscape is never far away.

Basel

A Creative City on the Rhine

Basel, the country's third-largest city, sits at the border between Switzerland, France and Germany, with the futuristic *Dreiländereck* monument marking the spot.

The Old Town is a labyrinth of lanes, medieval buildings and squares built around fountains, once the primary source of drinking water in the city. Start at the town hall, with its warm-red façade and fanciful frescoes, and head up to the Spalenberg district, packed with boutiques and galleries. *Stella Studio* specializes in midcentury furniture, while concept store *Joyne* stocks everything from sustainable soap to knitted tote bags. Next, walk over to the *Basler Münster* with its distinctive sandstone walls, spires and colored roof tiles. Scaling the cathedral's towers offers unrivaled panoramic views.

The city, famous for Art Basel, is a major art hub. The *Kunstmuseum Basel* spans the 15th century right up to the present day, with works by Monet, Van Gogh, Picasso and Swiss artist Taeuber-Arp. The *Paper Museum* is set in an old mill on the banks of a small canal. Head about 20 minutes outside the center for the *Fondation Beyeler*, home to the extensive private collection of Ernst and Hildy Beyeler, located in a Renzo Piano building.

Basel's food scene lends itself to laid-back evenings by the river, where *buvettes* (open-air cafés) line the banks in Kleinbasel. Not far away, *Volkshaus Basel* has an intimate courtyard for French-inspired classics, while *Consum Basel* pairs salami and cheese specialties with more than 100 wines. *St. Alban Stübli* has evolved from a neighborhood pub to a traditional Swiss restaurant offering refined classic cuisine such as hand-cut beef tartare with delicate pommes allumettes (matchstick fries). For alternative fine dining options, try *Matt & Elly*, where the set menu can be combined with beers from the restaurant's own microbrewery. And finally, for more local brews, head to *Volta Bräu* in the up-and-coming St. Johann district for freshly tapped dark lagers and hazy wheat beers.

Photo: Basel Tourismus

Lucerne

Two Banks, One Heart

Many visitors to Lucerne never make it past Chapel Bridge, where the Reuss River flows out to Lake Lucerne. Cross the river in either direction, though, and the city quickly shifts from landmarks to everyday life.

North of the river, the Old Town is quieter than expected. Side streets wind past vintage clothing stores and concept boutiques before opening onto frescoed squares like Weinmarkt, where tables spill out beneath painted façades. Locals linger over lunch along the river, watching the Reuss drift by, while nearby cafés transition from morning coffee to evening drinks without much fuss.

Neustadt, the city's "new town" across the water, moves to a different rhythm, as coffee roasters, bookstores and cultural spaces anchor daily life. *Kaffeekranz* roasts its own beans for a local following, while *Neubad*—a repurposed indoor aquatic center—hosts poetry slams and concerts inside its empty, tiled pool. A few streets over, wine bars and casual restaurants keep things unpretentious. Head to *GlouGlou* for natural wine and *Onkel Salamat* for Iranian plates.

Then there's the lake, Lucerne's constant. In warmer months, its shores are in motion with boats gliding out to surrounding villages, paddleboards skimming the surface and swimmers diving in at Seebad Luzern. But it's in winter that the city feels most distinctly its own.

As temperatures drop, Lucerne leans into the season. Locals book sauna boats to steam across the frigid lake in a floating wood-fired sanctuary or curl up in warm blankets on the *KKL Luzern Terrace* for views of the Old Town and seasonal activity on the square below. Christmas markets fill the squares with the scent of mulled wine and melted cheese, while *Lilu Light Festival Lucerne* in January transforms the city with colorful projections that ripple across façades and reflect off the lake.

Then comes Fasnacht. Beginning in the early hours on Thursday before Ash Wednesday, Lucerne erupts into organized chaos: brass bands, elaborate costumes and confetti transforming the streets into one of Switzerland's most exuberant celebrations. It's the city's way of saying goodbye to winter in the loudest possible way.

Ticino

Piazzas & Plunges

Through the Gotthard Massif along the longest train tunnel in the world, escape to a palm-treed region beloved when the weather elsewhere is not playing ball.

Ticino is Italian-speaking, with the best bits of Switzerland and Italy rolled into one. Good weather, clean streets and local trains that run like clockwork combine with Italian food and bustling town piazzas.

Free public transportation, thanks to the Ticino Ticket included in every hotel and campground stay, opens up the entire canton. Start by exploring the capital, Bellinzona, which comes alive on Saturdays when the market stalls set up beneath the city's medieval fortresses.

From there, head further south to Lugano, home to the *LAC* cultural center, shops and local gastronomic gems like *Grotto dei Pescatori*, accessible only by boat in summer. Begin your day with breakfast at *Maurie Concept*, a store-turned-café, before visiting *Tutto/Niente*, a listening bar, restaurant and record store built around one of only three custom OJAS x NNNN sound systems in the world. As you travel, look up. Local architect Mario Botta's influence appears in many iconic buildings, from the chapel on Mount Tamaro to *Fiore di Pietra* on Monte Generoso. On Lago Maggiore, Locarno hosts the *Locarno Film Festival* each summer and serves as the gateway to the valleys beyond.

The valleys of Maggia and Verzasca cut deep into the mountains. Stone villages built along each valley's glacial rivers create fairy-tale-like scenes for hikes, picnics and summer dips that feel more like cold plunges than relief from the heat. The quiet village of Sonogno awaits at the end of Verzasca, near the La Froda Waterfall, contrasting sharply with the Contra Dam at the valley's entrance, where, like James Bond, you can throw yourself off the walls.

No visit to Ticino is complete without sharing a meal around a granite table at *Grotto America*, ideally in the shade of a chestnut tree. Nearly every menu features long-braised meat, such as osso buco or brasato, served with either risotto or polenta. The restaurant is also the ideal spot to taste locally made cheese, washed down with a Ticino merlot served in a ceramic tazzino as tradition dictates. As the locals say: *La boca l'è mia straca se la sa mia da vaca*, or "The mouth isn't tired until it tastes of cow."

Saas-Fee/Saastal

High-Alpine Adventure, Year-Round

Surrounded by 18 peaks topping 13,000 feet, Saas-Fee and the Saas Valley deliver big-mountain drama in a refreshingly understated setting.

The village itself is entirely car-free, with electric shuttles navigating the streets, and its sustainability efforts run deep with hydropower-generated energy and a long-standing commitment to low-impact tourism.

Winter arrives early here. Thanks to the area's glacier terrain and high altitude, skiing typically starts in the beginning of November and runs through mid-April, making it a reliable choice for both early-season trips and spring escapes. Across the valley, 100 miles of slopes cater to all levels, from challenging descents in Saas-Fee to sunny, scenic runs in Saas-Grund and family-friendly areas in Saas-Almagell.

But this is more than a ski destination. Ride the underground funicular, the highest of its kind, up above 11,500 feet, where the world's highest revolving restaurant serves sweeping views across the Alps. In warmer months, the focus shifts to hiking, glacier trekking and alpine adventures, with trails and high-mountain routes revealing a breathtaking landscape. From the first overnight stay in summer and autumn, cable cars (except the Metro Alpin) and PostBus travel in the Saas Valley are included, allowing easy access to the valley and mountains throughout the stay.

There's a playful side, too. You can feed the marmot ground squirrels, while Wham! fans can follow a self-guided walk through the "Last Christmas" filming locations. More active visitors can opt for sunrise skiing, night-time biking, full-moon snowshoeing or a candlelit fondue dinner on a gondola.

Whether for snow, adventure or high-altitude thrills, Saas-Fee/Saastal offers an Alpine experience that feels both grand and surprisingly accessible.

Photo: SaastalTourismusAG-PuzzleMedia

Aletsch Arena

Switzerland's Quiet UNESCO Giant

If you want alpine drama without the crowds, the Aletsch Arena is one of Switzerland's best-kept secrets. This cluster of villages and mountain viewpoints sits beside the Aletsch Glacier, the longest glacier in the Alps and part of a UNESCO World Heritage landscape.

From certain lookouts, you can even spot a trio of icons—the Matterhorn, Jungfrau and Mont Blanc—all on the same horizon.

The region is refreshingly low-key. Several villages are car-free, cable cars run on renewable energy and the historic *Villa Cassel* has become a model for sustainable alpine tourism. Trails weave through the protected Aletsch Forest, where some trees are close to 1,000 years old, while guided treks (taking at least six hours) take more adventurous visitors across the glacier itself.

For a cultural detour, explore the *Aletsch Alpine Museum* in Riederalp, which brings local mountain traditions to life, including butter and cheesemaking workshops. Down in Brig, the grand *Stockalper Palace* offers a glimpse of the region's baroque past.

But the real charm lies in the slower details. Wander through quiet villages such as Betten or Fieschertal, cross the dramatic Goms Bridge or hike to hidden viewpoints like Märjela Lake. Afterward, settle in at *Chüestall*, once a cow stable, now a laid-back restaurant with big mountain views, and order a slice of *cholera*, a hearty Valais pie packed with potatoes, leeks, apples and cheese.

It's the kind of place locals describe as *hüero güet*, Valais dialect slang for "seriously good."

Val d'Anniviers/ Leukerbad

Val d'Anniviers: Alpine Traditions, Unfiltered

Tucked beneath a ring of 13,000-foot peaks known as the Couronne Impériale, Val d'Anniviers blends big-mountain scenery with a strong sense of local life. Summer and autumn are prime time: Hike sections of the Tour du Val d'Anniviers, wander easy bisse trails or head up to the striking Moiry Lake and dam. What sets the valley apart is its living traditions. You can try rye breadmaking, taste rare glacier wine aged high in the mountains or join a guided village walk that brings local history into focus. With free public transport included for overnight guests, it's easy to explore slowly and stumble into the small, everyday moments that give the valley its local feel.

Leukerbad: Soak, Ski, Repeat

High in the Valais Alps, Leukerbad strikes a balance between mountain energy and serious downtime. Days are all about the outdoors: skiing and sledging in winter, or hiking, biking and via ferrata routes in summer, with standout views from the Gemmi and Torrent peaks. Then come the baths. Around a million gallons of thermal water flow through the village daily, feeding steaming pools that are best enjoyed early in the morning or after sunset. Between gorge walks (don't miss Dala Gorge), spa sessions and long, relaxed dinners, Leukerbad settles into an easy rhythm. It's equal parts alpine adventure and full reset.

Photos: © Sierre-Anniviers Marketing, © MyLeukerbad AG

Region Dents du Midi/ Martigny/Nendaz

Region Dents du Midi: Big Terrain, Local Soul

On the Swiss-French border, the Region Dents du Midi pairs alpine playgrounds with Valais character. As part of Les Portes du Soleil (one of the world's largest ski areas), it offers 400 miles of slopes and 500 miles of hiking across the full domain, yet villages like Champéry and Morgins keep things down to earth. In warmer months, the 34-mile Tour des Dents du Midi circles jagged peaks and high alpine passes. Year-round, it's a place for big views and simple pleasures like savoring lunch in a mountain cantine or crossing into France on foot.

Nendaz: Big Ski, Local Feel

In the heart of the 4 Vallées, Nendaz delivers access to more than 250 miles of pistes, the largest fully Swiss ski area, with terrain for first-timers and seasoned skiers alike. For the full wow factor, head up to Mont Fort, where views stretch from the Matterhorn to Mont Blanc, with a zipline for extra adrenaline. Off the slopes, things slow down. Think snowshoe hikes with raclette over an open fire, spa sessions and village traditions. Come summer, historic bisse trails and mountain paths take over with the same sweeping views, just greener.

Martigny Region: Where the South Begins

At the crossroads of Switzerland, France and Italy, Martigny blends alpine scenery with softer, sun-soaked vibes. Spring to autumn is prime time: Walk through vineyards in Plan-Cerisier, explore the dramatic Durnand Gorge or ride up to Emosson for big-mountain views. Culture runs deep, too, from the sculpture park at the Fondation Pierre Gianadda to the historic St-Maurice Abbey nearby. Add in distillery stops, thermal baths and easy valley walks, and you've got a region that's as relaxed as it is varied.

Photos: Christian David Wikimedia CC BY-SA 4.0, Lévy Loye, © Martigny Tourisme

Swiss
Travel Pass
One Ticket, All of Switzerland

In most countries, transit is simply the friction between destinations. In Switzerland, it's part of the journey.

You cross alpine passes, hug shoreline curves and glide over glacial lakes without ever touching a steering wheel. The public transport system is one of the most comprehensive in the world, and the Swiss Travel Pass unlocks this 20,000-mile network, turning trains, buses, boats and mountain railways into a seamless, car-free ecosystem. This freedom reshapes how you experience the country.

The Swiss Travel Pass offers unlimited travel for 3, 4, 6, 8 or 15 days, either consecutive or flexible, eliminating the need for rigid itineraries. You simply move. You might start the morning with an espresso in lakeside Lucerne, board a panoramic train by noon and find yourself deep in the Alps by evening. If a village catches your eye, step off the train, wander and continue on to the next connection.

At the heart of the network is the Grand Train Tour of Switzerland (see page 34), the ultimate Swiss rail journey rolling the most famous panoramic lines into one round trip. These include the GoldenPass Express, Gotthard Panorama Express, Bernina Express, Glacier Express and Luzern–Interlaken Express. Seat reservations are required for several of these routes due to their popularity. Beyond the famous five, quieter lines like the Vigezzina-Centovalli Railway and Voralpen-Express deliver stunning scenery with a fraction of the crowds. Or for something more playful, try a culinary route with fun themes like cheese, chocolate or cookies.

The pass also grants access to boats that drift across lakes like Geneva and Lucerne, cogwheel railways that climb into the high Alps, and buses like the iconic yellow PostBus that wind over mountain passes. Excursions to peaks such as Rigi, Stoos and Stanserhorn are included, while many others come at reduced rates. Along the way, more than 500 museums and attractions like Thun Castle are free to enter, adding cultural depth to the journey.

In addition to reducing logistics, travel on the pass reduces your environmental impact. One-hundred percent of Swiss trains run on renewable energy, making public transport the most sustainable way to explore the country.

One essential tip: Download the Swiss Federal Railways (SBB) app. Every train, bus, boat and gondola is listed, with door-to-door planning in real time. And for those bringing the next generation of explorers, the Swiss Family Card ensures children under 16 travel free alongside a parent.

• Swiss Travel Pass, myswitzerland.com/tickets

Photos: Patrick Robert Doyle, Countdan

Grand Train Tour of Switzerland

One Track, Infinite Wonders

For more than a decade, the Grand Train Tour of Switzerland has connected the country's most impressive railway routes into a single grand journey available throughout the year. The route threads through alpine hubs, sunny valleys and spectacular mountain passes.

Spanning nearly 800 miles, this eight-stage circuit serves as a staggering inventory of the Swiss landscape. The round-trip journey includes 11 major lakes, four linguistic regions and five UNESCO World Heritage Sites. It is a journey of contrast, from the crisp waters of Lake Constance to the palm trees of Ticino, threading through serene villages and historic towns along the way.

The standard itinerary spans eight days and seven nights, starting and finishing in Zurich, yet the structure remains entirely flexible. You can join the circuit at any point, combining or shortening stages to suit your pace. Like the road-based version (see page 8), the Grand Train Tour of Switzerland is a fully bookable rail product, available either as a complete package or in segments. For those with less time, compact options are available, such as the five-day Top Attractions Tour or the four-day Glaciers & Palm Trees experience.

The journey is defined by five legendary panoramic trains featuring floor-to-ceiling windows. The slow-rolling Glacier Express links Zermatt and St. Moritz, traversing high-altitude bridges and long tunnels to showcase the full scale of the Alps. The Bernina Express climbs the mountains without the aid of a rack-and-pinion system, following the UNESCO-listed route of the Rhaetian Railway. Elsewhere, the GoldenPass Express stretches from the Bernese Oberland to the shores of Vaud, while the Luzern–Interlaken Express connects two distinct lakeside worlds. Completing the famous five, the Gotthard Panorama Express pairs a historic rail route over the Gotthard Pass with a scenic steamboat cruise across Lake Lucerne. Seat reservations are mandatory for the Glacier Express, Bernina Express and Gotthard Panorama Express and recommended for the others.

World-famous photo ops await along the way: the rugged terrain of Jungfrau, the Matterhorn rising above Zermatt, the medieval Chillon Castle on Lake Geneva, the Chapel Bridge in Lucerne and the thundering Rhine Falls near Schaffhausen. Two architectural marvels have become stars in their own right: the Landwasser Viaduct near Filisur and the circular Brusio Viaduct, both highlights of the Rhaetian Railway.

A physical travel booklet serves as your companion, offering a place to collect station stamps and log personal impressions. It's packed with local lore and fun facts designed to sharpen your

Photo: Oskar Gross

eye for the details others might overlook. If you prefer a digital guide, the app provides real-time push notifications, ensuring you never miss a hidden detour or panoramic view as it approaches your window.

Switzerland boasts one of the world's most extensive and punctual transit networks, engineered with the philosophy that the journey is never secondary to the destination. The Grand Train Tour of Switzerland acts as a continuous thread, stitching together dramatic landscapes, Swiss engineering and local life into one seamless loop. It offers a comfortable, sustainable path through the country's most incomparable facets, proving that the most authentic way to see Switzerland is to move with it.

For full itinerary details and real-time navigation, Switzerland Tourism provides comprehensive resources. International visitors can also purchase a multiday Swiss Travel Pass (see page 32) to unlock the entire network of trains, buses and boats.

• grandtraintour.com

GOLDENPASS
EXPRESS

GoldenPass Express

Mountains Meet the Riviera

Imagine waking up to crisp mountain air and spending your afternoon strolling a palm-lined promenade. The GoldenPass Express makes this transition effortless, connecting the rugged heart of the Alps to the sunny Montreux Riviera in a seamless 3-hour, 15-minute journey.

Since its debut in December 2022, this engineering marvel has linked Interlaken Ost and Montreux with four daily departures in each direction. The train line includes towns like Spiez, Zweisimmen, Gstaad, Saanen and Château-d'Oex, with two different track sizes. A world-first track-switching system allows the train to adjust its gauge and height automatically, eliminating the need for a transfer.

The scenery is a rotating gallery of Swiss icons: the blue glints of Lake Thun, the timber houses of the Simmental and the mountainous meadows of Gstaad. As the train descends toward Lake Geneva, the landscape shifts from dramatic peaks to terraced vineyards and local flora. Along the way, you cross the Röstigraben, the invisible cultural and linguistic frontier between German- and French-speaking Switzerland.

The experience on board is defined by your choice of perspective. Prestige Class features heated, swiveling leather seats that always face the direction of travel and sit 15 inches higher than those in first and second class. Even in the standard cabins, floor-to-ceiling panoramic windows ensure you are fully immersed in the shifting seasons. The journey is also a culinary experience. You can pre-order regional appetizer platters, Swiss caviar or breakfast boxes, paired with crisp Lavaux wine, Gstaad cheese or craft beer from Interlaken.

The route is covered by the Swiss Travel Pass, but seat reservations are mandatory for Prestige Class and recommended for other classes. For those who prefer a touch of history, the GoldenPass Belle Époque runs on select stretches of this line, offering the charm of the Orient Express against a backdrop of alpine peaks.

- GoldenPass Express, gpx.swiss
- GoldenPass Belle Epoque, mob.ch

Photo: ©Switzerland_Tourism-André_Meier

Glacier Express

Slow and Scenic

The Glacier Express doesn't rush anywhere. And that's exactly the point.

Often called the world's slowest express train, it glides through the Swiss Alps at a pace that encourages you to settle in, relax and simply watch the landscape unfold beyond its panoramic windows. The scenery shifts constantly along the way. In winter, the high alpine world is blanketed in snow. In summer, valleys turn lush and green, dotted with wildflowers and wooden chalets. Spring and autumn bring softer light and quieter colors as clouds drift low over the mountains and the changing weather reshapes the view from one moment to the next. It's one of those journeys where the outside world feels like a moving postcard.

Food is part of the experience, too. The Glacier Express is the only train in Switzerland where meals are freshly prepared onboard during the journey. Regional dishes are served right at your seat, so you can enjoy your lunch and a tilted glass of wine as glaciers and forests roll past the windows. Seasoned travelers know the best moments often happen between the big photo stops. Watch how the light shifts across a mountainside, notice the sudden change from high alpine terrain to quiet valleys or spot the contrast between the snowy peaks and blooming flowers far below.

This is a trip best enjoyed at an unhurried pace, ideally with a good view and something delicious on your plate. Note that both a valid travel ticket and a seat reservation are required for the Glacier Express, and booking in advance is recommended.

• glacierexpress.ch

Photos: @ Titlis Cableways, © Glacier Express – Stefan Schlumpf

Titlis Cableways

Big Views, Fresh Altitude

Open year-round, Titlis Cableways is one of Central Switzerland's most accessible high-alpine hits, and it's evolving fast. The journey itself is a spectacle with the Titlis Rotair, the world's first revolving cable car, which offers a 360-degree panorama as you ascend. The trip culminates on the glacier at more than 10,000 feet, where snow is a permanent fixture, and views stretch deep into the heart of the Alps.

A major new chapter for the summit arrived with the *Titlis Tower*, a striking landmark designed by Herzog & de Meuron that opened in May 2026. The project transformed an existing 1980s steel postal tower into a cross-shaped structure, with four horizontal glazed beams that appear to float above the ice. The top beams house an upscale restaurant and a separate bar/lounge, while the lower section is home to a Rolex boutique. The transformation continues further down the mountain, where there is a new restaurant named *Atelier Hess*.

Winter at Titlis brings a playful edge, from racing electric snowmobiles at *SnowXpark* to fondue and mulled wine inside an igloo. In warmer months, the energy shifts to Lake Trübsee for lakeside walks and rowing. Locals keep it simple here, often spending Sundays at the public fireplaces, grilling in the crisp mountain air by the waters. It's a classic Swiss mountain outing, now recharged with world-class architecture and a fresh jolt of energy.

• Engelberg, titlis.ch

Schilthorn Cableway

Steep Thrills, Understated Heights

Autumn is when the journey to the Schilthorn feels especially magical. The air sharpens and the crowds thin, revealing a landscape where time seems to pause.

Even before reaching the summit, the ascent delivers a once-in-a-lifetime experience. The new cable car between Stechelberg and Mürren is the steepest aerial cableway in the world, climbing dramatically up sheer rock faces. From Mürren to Birg and onward to the Schilthorn, state-of-the-art cabins glide toward a brand-new station perched at nearly 10,000 feet.

The architecture of the renewed summit station blends carefully into the surrounding UNESCO World Heritage landscape, proving that contemporary design and high alpine nature can coexist. Inside, wide viewing windows frame the Eiger, Mönch and Jungfrau like living paintings. Surrounded by more than 200 alpine peaks, the revolving *Piz Gloria* restaurant turns slowly to reveal the panorama as you enjoy breakfast or lunch.

Below the summit lies the car-free village of Mürren, home to around 400 residents. Life here moves at cable car speed and no faster. There are no engines, only boots on wooden walkways and cowbells from distant pastures.

The village is home to the world's oldest and largest amateur ski race (The Inferno) and Switzerland's oldest palace hotel (the 19th-century Hotel Mürren Palace). Sustainability shapes daily operations, too, with innovative energy systems powering the cable cars, stations and *Hotel Alpenruh*, a chalet-style property delivering epic views of the region's famous mountains.

Throughout the seasons, the region invites adventure. Hiking routes cross alpine meadows, and a via ferrata route traces the cliffs in summer. Tandem paragliders drift above waterfalls such as the mighty Mürrenbach, and winter brings pristine ski slopes. Yet what lingers most is the quiet. In Mürren, surrounded by peaks, you rediscover the luxury of never being in a rush.

• Stechelberg, schilthorn.ch

SWISS

Fully Connected

In a country shaped by rugged verticality, Swiss International Air Lines (SWISS) has elevated transit to an art form. By integrating its flight routes into the national rail network, the airline offers a seamless air-rail connection that remains one of Switzerland's best-kept travel secrets.

The system is elegantly simple. With SWISS Air Rail, you can book a flight to Switzerland and an onward train journey with a single ticket. Headed to Grindelwald? Your air ticket continues the journey via Swiss Federal Railways (SBB), delivering you deep into the Alps without needing a rental car or second check-in. Skis and snowboards fly free of charge, and passengers can upgrade their baggage delivery through AirPortr, a SWISS partner, which sends your bags directly to their final destination.

U.S. travelers need to be aware of these services since they'll likely be flying SWISS anyway. As one might expect, the national carrier has the most nonstop flights between Switzerland and the U.S., including major gateway cities like New York, Los Angeles, Boston, Chicago, San Francisco, Miami and Washington, D.C.

The flight schedule focuses on global routes, but the onboard experience stays local with a cultural preview of the destination. SWISS Taste of Switzerland, its long-haul culinary program, features rotating regional menus, often created in collaboration with Michelin-starred chefs. This can include vegetarian dishes from Hiltl, the world's oldest vegetarian restaurant. Premium cabins showcase Swiss craftsmanship with Zimmerli sleepwear and VIU amenity kits, while every passenger receives a signature Swiss chocolate before arrival.

Those prone to jet lag will appreciate an emphasis on well-being through the SWISS Senses experience. By pairing circadian-synced lighting with a signature Alpine Valley scent by natural cosmetics house Soeder, SWISS eases the transition across time zones.

Taken together, services like rail integration, regional cuisine, sensory cabin environments, extensive global routes and premium baggage delivery are a blueprint for a better trip. Factor them in before you book, and they might change how you plan your journey.

• swiss.com

Photos: Leila Azevedo, Devam Jhabak

Jungfraujoch

Top of Europe

Swiss engineering reveals one of its greatest triumphs at 11,332 feet, where a ribbon of steel pierces a jagged saddle of rock and ice. Welcome to *Jungfraujoch - Top of Europe*, the highest railway station in Europe and the result of a near-mythic clash between human resolve and alpine extremes.

Photos: Patrick Robert Doyle, Daniel R.

The project began in 1896, and for nearly two decades, workers carved a tunnel through the heart of the Eiger and Mönch under high-altitude conditions. What was once a feat of endurance is now a cinematic ascent, the final stretch unfolding almost entirely within the mountain itself.

At the summit, the station opens into a vast complex overlooking the Aletsch Glacier, the longest river of ice in the Alps. It feels otherworldly. Tunnels lead to ice palaces carved directly into the glacier, while the outdoor plateau puts you eye-level with the frozen expanse. Crowning it all is the Sphinx

Observatory, a silver-domed research station equipped with a 30-inch telescope and engineered to withstand cold, violent winds. A high-speed lift rockets you more than 350 feet through solid rock in seconds, delivering visitors to the Sphinx terrace. To the south, the glacier spills outward in a slow, frozen tide. To the north, the land drops away toward the Swiss Plateau, with views reaching as far as Germany's Black Forest on a clear day.

This is a place of sharp contrasts. Even in summer, the air often bites with freezing intensity, a stark counterpoint to the green valleys below. Yet beyond the spectacle, the Sphinx is a working research station, its altitude and clarity making it ideal for monitoring atmospheric conditions, cosmic radiation and the fragile pulse of the surrounding glaciers.

Jungfraujoch endures as a testament to Swiss ingenuity. It's proof that no rock is too high or too hard when a country has peak ambition.

• Bernese Alps, jungfrau.ch

Scenic Cycling

Switzerland on Two Wheels

Switzerland is a cyclist's playground, where every ride comes with a side of jaw-dropping scenery.

For a gentler pace, you can follow the Lakes Route, winding along Lake Geneva, Lake Constance and others, passing vineyards, castles and charming towns, or trace the Rhône from its glacier-fed source through the Valais valley down to Geneva. For a wilder backdrop, the Rhine Route threads through the dramatic Ruinaulta, known as Switzerland's Grand Canyon, before spilling into Basel, with towering cliffs and rushing waters lining your ride.

For those chasing altitude and challenge, alpine roads deliver climbs that reward every pedal stroke. The Furka–Grimsel–Susten Loop threads three legendary passes, with glaciers forming a breathtaking backdrop to every twisting switchback. Gotthard Pass rises steeply through high valleys and rocky ridges, offering long climbs and sweeping panoramas over the surrounding peaks. Slightly more remote and less trafficked, Grosse Scheidegg ascends quietly into alpine meadows, framed by the iconic Eiger, Mönch and Jungfrau. Quiet valleys, hairpins and high-altitude vistas make each ride as exhilarating as the scenery itself.

Off-road riders will find endless playgrounds in Switzerland's forests, valleys and alpine trails. For those chasing speed, Lenzerheide offers flowing singletracks and lift-assisted downhill runs, while Arosa's trails mix technical alpine climbs with rocky descents, ideal for building skill and endurance. In Flims-Laax, wide alpine meadows give way to switchbacks and natural jumps, pairing panoramic views with playful terrain. From beginner-friendly tracks to more demanding descents, the Swiss mountains offer something for every rider looking to venture beyond the paved road.

• Various locations

Mount Pilatus

The Dragon's Peak

Scale the Summit

Medieval legend claims dragons once roamed the mountaintop, but most visitors arrive to the 6,983-foot Pilatus the traditional way: the Golden Round Trip with a boat from Lucerne, the world's steepest cog railway climb, and the descent on a panoramic cable car. To fully experience the mountain, stay overnight at the historic *Hotel Pilatus-Kulm*, operating on the summit since 1890. While there, indulge in fondue at *Restaurant Pilatus-Kulm* or explore the mountain's past in the exhibit along the corridor connecting the hotel.

• Lucerne, pilatus.ch

Ride the Dragon

In warmer months, hike the flower trail to Tomlishorn, the highest point in the Pilatus range. Along the way, watch for gravity-defying alpine ibex—the wild mountain goats you've probably seen online scaling near-vertical rock faces with ease. Or take flight on the "Dragon Ride," an aerial cableway designed like a helicopter cockpit. Upon arrival in Fräkmüntegg, extend the thrill on the Dragon Glider that lets you soar through the forest canopy. Tree tents suspended in the forest near Fräkmüntegg offer a different kind of immersion.

Winter Magic

When the first snow settles, a quiet magic takes hold. Think hushed landscapes, a decorated panorama gallery and sipping Swiss hot chocolate. December brings a festive glow, where Christmas carols, traditional cookies and the scent of gingerbread and spiced wine drift in the mountain breeze. If conditions allow, follow the Dragon Path through rock passages where carved openings frame the peaks beyond. For the most tranquil experience, come early in the year when it's often just you and perhaps an alpine chough gliding overhead.

Photos: Simon von Dach, Stefan Schlumpf

Leo Luminati

Where the Mountains Feel Like Home

There's a certain type of mountain guide you come across in the Alps: experienced, instinctive and more comfortable moving through snow and rock than talking about it. Leo Luminati is exactly that. Born and raised in St. Moritz, he grew up skiing the Engadin long before it became synonymous with winter glamour. Today, he works as a mountain guide and off-piste instructor, leading clients through terrain most would never attempt alone. His work has taken him far beyond

Switzerland, to remote regions like Tajikistan, and he also operates as a helicopter rescue specialist with the Swiss Air Rescue Guard (REGA), an experience that has fundamentally shaped how he thinks about risk in the mountains. Despite that résumé, he remains disarmingly down-to-earth. Spend a little time talking to him, and what comes through isn't bravado, but an elemental clarity about the landscape, people and the fine line between pushing limits and knowing when to turn back.

You grew up in St. Moritz. What did a typical winter look like for you as a kid?

It was very simple, actually, just a lot of snow and a lot of skiing. And a bit of school in between. I also played hockey when I was younger, but at a certain point I had to choose. It wasn't possible to continue both at the same level, and skiing just stayed. Being outside all the time, moving in the mountains, that was always the main thing.

What keeps drawing you back to the Engadin?

It's a feeling. When I drive over the Julier Pass and reach the top, and I see Piz Bernina, the Bianco Ridge and the lake, it's just home. It's hard to explain, but it's something I feel every time. I've seen many beautiful places, really impressive mountains, but here it's different. The valley is open, the light is special, and everything is quite close. Especially in spring. You can ski in the morning, then drive down to Italy and go climbing in the sun, have a cappuccino. It's a very good balance.

How would you describe your work to someone who's never spent time in the mountains?

I would say I bring people to places they wouldn't go alone, and I show them a bit of my world. In the mountains, there are not really fixed rules like in everyday life, but you still need rules. You create them yourself so that you come back home safely. That's the most important part.

What separates a good mountain guide from a great one?

It's more complex than just finding good snow. You have to understand the terrain, the wind, how the snow has been affected, how the layers are built. It's always changing, so you need to read it carefully. But at the same time, you work with people. And that's maybe just as important. Sometimes clients say they want to do something difficult, like a steep face, but actually they just want to enjoy a beautiful day. Not everyone can express that clearly. So a big part of the job is understanding what they really want, even if they don't say it directly.

So it's also about reading people?

Yes, very much. You look at how they move, how tired they are, how confident they feel. It's not only about what they say. And this also makes it safer, for them and for me.

Besides being a mountain guide, you work in helicopter rescue with REGA. How has that influenced you?

It changed my perspective a lot. When you go on rescues, you see what can happen in the mountains. You see avalanches, accidents, situations where things went wrong. After each one, you try to understand why. That experience makes you more aware. You become more careful, more reflective. It's not just theoretical anymore: You've seen it.

What do people misunderstand about off-piste skiing?

Many people think it's always very dangerous because they only hear about accidents. But in reality, there are quite simple rules. For example, avalanches usually need a certain steepness: over about 30 degrees. If you stay below that, and you choose your terrain carefully, it can be very safe. Most of the time, nothing happens. But that part is not in the news.

How do you prepare for a more serious day in the mountains?

It starts before you even go out. You check the weather, the terrain, the conditions.

Then once you're outside, you check again, because forecasts are not always perfect. You compare what you see with what you expected. We also communicate a lot between guides. We share photos, information, warnings about certain slopes or conditions. It's quite a strong network, and it helps everyone make better decisions.

That sounds like a strong community.

Yes, it is. We ski together, climb together, travel together. It's not only work. We spend time together outside of it, going climbing in Greece or Sardinia, for example.

It's a small community. Maybe you could say we are a bit like modern hippies.

You've skied the "Free Fall" in St. Moritz, which is known for being the steepest start in the world. What does it feel like at the top?

When you stand there and look down, it feels extremely steep. As a skier, you always have this instinct of wanting to try it. But once you start, you realize very quickly how fast it is. Skiing straight is one thing, but as soon as you begin to turn, you feel the forces much more. That's when you really understand the speed.

How do you deal with fear in those situations?

I don't try to block it. I feel it, and I use it. Fear makes me more focused. It sharpens everything. In normal life, I'm maybe not always so concentrated, but when there is risk, I become very focused and precise. In that way, it actually helps.

Veltlinerkeller
St. Moritz

Scarpetta
St. Moritz

Suvretta House
St. Moritz

What did competition skiing teach you that guiding doesn't?

Competition is very different. There is only one winner, and everything is focused on that. In guiding, it's not like this. If everyone goes up and comes back safely, that's success.

But competition teaches you something important: that if you want to be the best at something, you have to give everything. It's not just a part of your life, it's your whole life.

You've also taken part in the White Turf races, the horse races held each winter on the frozen lake of St. Moritz. What are they like from a local perspective?

For locals, it's something special because everyone is there. On those days, the slopes are empty, and the whole town is on the lake. And even if you don't have the best horse, people support you. You feel it when you walk out. It's a really nice atmosphere.

What would you recommend to someone visiting St. Moritz who doesn't want to ski every day?

For me, it's always something active. But something simple that I really enjoy is ice skating on one of the frozen lakes, especially when there's no snow and the ice is clear. You just glide, without effort. It's very quiet and very special.

And in summer?

Summer is beautiful. You can hike to a small lake, swim and then maybe paraglide down into the valley. It has also become busier in recent years, especially in August, because it's so hot in the cities. But the landscape, the colors, the light, it's really amazing.

Do you have a favorite area nearby?

Val Bregaglia, on the way to Italy. The granite there is incredible. Places like Soglio, too. It's a very small village, maybe 100 or 150 people. It feels very quiet, almost like another time.

And a favorite hike?

I like the one to the Segantini Hut. It's not a long hike, maybe a couple of hours, but it's absolutely beautiful.

Where do you go for a good, simple meal?

If I want something traditional, I go to *Veltlinerkeller* for pizzoccheri. I also really like a restaurant called *Scarpetta*. It's a small place, but they make everything themselves. It's simple, but very good.

And to relax after a long day?

There are some very nice spas in St. Moritz, like the one in *Suvretta House*. After a long day outside, that's always a good way to recover.

You've seen a lot of Switzerland. Are there places you return to again and again?

Zermatt. I spend a lot of time there, as many tours start from the village. The Matterhorn is such an important peak for us in Switzerland, and having it so close always feels special.

And is there anywhere in the country that still feels undiscovered to you?

I would say Wendenstöcke in the Bernese Alps. I went climbing there once and was awestruck. It felt like a completely new world. I think about going back a lot, though with friends, not clients, as it's actually quite hard climbing.

After everything you've done, what keeps it exciting for you?

I really love my life. I wouldn't change it. Being outside, moving in nature. That's enough.

• **stmoritz-mountainguides.ch**

Walk the Edge

Perched above the car-free village of Stoos, the ridge trail from Klingenstock to Fronalpstock is a hike that lives up to its hype. Kick things off with a ride on the world's steepest funicular, with a vertical climb to Stoos that's a thrill in its own right. For two and a half hours, you'll follow the narrow ridge trail with sheer drops on either side, while 360-degree views stretch across more than 10 Swiss lakes and iconic peaks like Pilatus, Rigi and the Mythen. At Fronalpstock, a viewing platform and restaurant reward you with stunning vistas over Lake Lucerne, the perfect spot to toast your adventure before riding the chairlift down.

- Stoos Ridge Hike, Stoos, stoos.ch/en/stories/stoos-ridge-hike

Outdoors

Chase the Elements

From thundering waterfalls to glacier-carved depths, Switzerland delivers nature at full volume. This is a landscape built for movement, where every trail, drop and ridgeline turns the outdoors into a visceral adventure.

The Narrow Path

Along a dramatic limestone chasm in the Haslital valley, the Aare Gorge reveals nature at full force. Over millennia, the glacial-blue Aare River has carved a passage through 650-foot cliffs, narrowing to just a few feet in places. Light filters down in shifting bands, casting the gorge in shadow, color and echo. Wooden walkways and rock tunnels cling to the walls, where cool mist rises and water thunders below. It's an easy, awe-inspiring walk through a landscape sculpted by scale, force and time.

- Aare Gorge, Meiringen, aareschlucht.ch

Photos: © Glacier0000, Patrick Robert Doyle

Peak Velocity

Set high above the Rhône Valley, the *Mont 4 Zipline* offers one of the most exhilarating ways to take in the Alps. Starting near Mont Fort, it stretches nearly a mile, sending riders flying across open mountain terrain at speeds that can top 60 miles per hour. Suspended between sky and valley, the experience is less about adrenaline alone and more about the sheer scale of the landscape unfolding beneath you: glaciers, peaks and steep drops in every direction. It's a quick hit of altitude, speed and perspective all at once on one of the world's highest ziplines.

• **Mont 4 Zipline, verbier4vallees.ch**

Lake Life

Swimming in Switzerland isn't on everyone's radar, but it should be. Home to more than 1,500 lakes, there is almost always somewhere to swim within easy reach, even in the mountains. Around Flims and Laax, three experiences await. Caumasee draws the crowds with its turquoise waters on hot weekends. Crestasee (photo) is the locals' secret tucked in the forest nearby. For the most adventurous, hike high into alpine meadows to Alp Mora and swim in the naturally carved glacial rock pools. Cold, clear and worth every step.

• **Various locations**

Into the Blue

Opportunities to step inside a living glacier are rare, and the Rhône Glacier Ice Cave offers exactly that. A short walk from the famous Furka Pass leads to a 300-foot tunnel carved anew each summer to compensate for the glacier's rapid melting, revealing layers of blue and white ice built up over decades. Along the translucent corridors, small crevices and smooth walls trace the glacier's slow movement, glowing with natural, ethereal light. At 7,500 feet above sea level, the experience puts you face-to-face with the power and fragile beauty of the High Alps.

• **Rhône Glacier Ice Cave, valais.ch**

Around the Horn

Switzerland is packed with world-class ski and snowboard resorts, each with its own appeal, but Zermatt stands out for its combination of scenery and scale. The Matterhorn rises dramatically over the slopes, while high-altitude glacier terrain makes skiing and snowboarding possible year-round. From cruising wide pistes and hitting snow parks to freeride lines, ski touring or even heliskiing for the boldest, there's a run for every style, with slopes that sweep across the border into Italy. Off the slopes, lively après-ski spots keep the energy going well into the evening, rounding out one of the Alps' most complete snow experiences.

• **Zermatt, zermatt.swiss**

River Riders

The lakeside town of Thun is not the first place that comes to mind for surfing. Yet, below its 18th-century wooden bridges spanning the Aare River, a standing wave of water rushing from Lake Thun draws experienced surfers to the heart of the city. Known as the Flusswelle, the wave is powerful enough to challenge seasoned riders, with two distinct spots offering different levels of difficulty. Even watching the spectacle from the bridge is worth the trip, but if you want to try it yourself, beginner courses run throughout the season.

• Flusswelle, Aare River, Thun

James Bond Jump

Few film stunts are as iconic as the opening jump in *GoldenEye*, when James Bond launches himself from the towering Contra Dam. The 700-foot plunge is widely considered one of cinema's greatest stunts, and you can actually try it yourself. Suspended high above the emerald waters of the Verzasca Valley, the dam is a striking feat of engineering with sweeping views over Ticino's rugged landscape. Thrill-seekers can book the 007 Jump, leaping from the platform for a 7.5-second free fall on one of the highest bungee jumps in the world.

• 007 Bungee Jump, Contra Dam (Diga Verzasca), Ticino

Full Throttle

An alpine adrenaline playground, *SnowXpark* flips winter fun on its head. Gather your friends and choose your ride. Race across circuits on the Moon-Bike, the world's first electric snowbike, drift tight corners on an e-Snowmobile or charge down the slopes on a Bobsla, a compact hybrid of bob and snowmobile. For those looking to push the day further, take a ride up toward Mount Titlis to the *Titlis Cliff Walk*, a suspended bridge spanning a 1,640-foot abyss and offering dizzying panoramic views, making SnowXpark the starting point for a full-throttle, scenic winter adventure.

• SnowXpark, Trübsee, titlis.ch/en/activities/snowxpark

Feel the Rush

Europe's largest waterfall by volume, the Rhine Falls is a spectacle of sheer power and scale. Every second, more than 150,000 gallons of the Rhine thunder down a 75-foot drop. The result is a 500-foot-wide wall of water that kicks up a silver mist that shimmers in the sunlight. A wooden walkway and platforms stretch toward the Mittelfelsen, the solitary rock at the falls' center, while boat trips let you experience the rushing waters from the river itself. Panoramic trails, lifts and adventure paths trace the gorge from multiple angles, revealing the river's raw energy and the dramatic ice-age geology that shaped this natural spectacle over millennia.

• Rhine Falls, Schaffhausen, rheinfall.ch/en

Sonic Trails

Switzerland's pristine trails and panoramic mountain vistas are legendary, but in Toggenburg, hiking comes with a twist. Developed by the Klangwelt Toggenburg Foundation, the Sound Trail winds from Alp Sellamatt past Iltios to Oberdorf, featuring 27 sound-art installations by Swiss and international artists in conversation with the landscape. Passing through forests, meadows, alpine slopes and lakes, you can experiment with chimes, bells, wooden resonators and other interactive sculptures, or pause at listening stations that amplify and reveal the region's soundscapes. Open late May through October, the trail turns a hike into an immersive auditory adventure.

• Sound Trail, Toggenburg, klangwelt.ch/en/locations/sound-trail

Painting the Alps

With an entire Swiss canton as its walls, Art Valais is an open-air museum unlike any other. Founded by artist Jasm One, it has already placed more than 100 murals by celebrated Swiss and international artists across Valais, an alpine territory covering 2,000 square miles. Each work is rooted in local identity, as artists are invited to stay in the region and research their chosen village. In Eischoll, Jasm One's own *Lichtblume* mural celebrates a rare alpine flower found almost nowhere else in Switzerland. The museum is free and navigable via a dedicated app.

• Art Valais Open Air Museum, artvalais.com

Shops

Sharp Swiss Style

From heritage denim and handmade chocolates to retail chalets and recycling pioneers, these are the brands and boutiques shaping modern Swiss craftsmanship. Some have been around for generations, with one shop selling Swiss Army knives since the 19th century.

Seasonal Chocolate

Named after the founder's chocolate-loving son, *Max Chocolatier* is a small Lucerne atelier where Swiss chocolate is treated with near-obsessive care. Everything is handmade in small batches using natural ingredients, with seasonal flavors changing throughout the year, and production kept deliberately small to ensure freshness. The boutique on Hertensteinstrasse is the place to browse silky pralines and inventive flavor combinations, but the real highlight is behind the scenes. At the nearby atelier, visitors can book intimate workshops, from truffle-stamping sessions to hands-on tastings, that offer a glimpse into the craft of a Swiss chocolatier. Just be sure to reserve ahead: Spots fill up fast.

• Max Chocolatier, Hertensteinstrasse 7, Lucerne, maxchocolatier.com

Chalet Shopping

Open daily year-round, *Landquart Fashion Outlet* brings more than 170+ designer, sports and lifestyle brands together across 100+ stores, with discounts of up to 70 percent. Designed like a traditional Swiss chalet village, this open-air destination pairs shopping with cafés, food trucks and restaurants, making it an easy place to spend a day. A recent expansion added a wider mix of brands and brought more diversity to its dining scene. Just 10 minutes from Chur and directly beside Landquart station (three minutes on foot), it's also the gateway to Laax, Davos and St. Moritz.

• Landquart Fashion Outlet, Alpenblick 5, Landquart, landquartfashionoutlet.ch

True Originals

In squeaky-clean Zurich, one shopkeeper isn't afraid to get a bit of indigo dye on his hands. Roger Hatt first brought Japanese denim pioneer Evisu to the city decades ago. Now celebrating its 40th year, *VMC Original* is a cult destination for those seeking timeless heritage and rugged durability. It is known throughout the city and beyond for its curated range of vintage-inspired jeans, heavy leather jackets and welted boots, much of its stock from Europe and Japan. In an age of fast fashion, VMC believes the best pieces are the ones that only get better with age.

• VMC Original, Rindermarkt 8, Kreis 1, vmcoriginal.com

Precision in Motion

Few brands embody Swiss precision as consistently as Victorinox. For nearly 150 years, the company has defined functional design with world-famous gear like the Original Swiss Army Knife, a compact icon of versatility. Today, that same philosophy extends into travel gear, where clean design meets purposeful functionality and meticulous attention to detail.

Designed and engineered in Switzerland with active lifestyles in mind, Victorinox Travel Gear stands out for its intelligent organization, durable materials and smooth-rolling wheels made to take on everything from cobbled old towns to crowded train stations. The products balance form and function in a way that feels distinctly Swiss: efficient, reliable and built to last.

From pocket knives and luggage to watches and kitchen tools, you can check out the full range of products at the Victorinox Flagship Store Zurich. Located in the heart of the city, the store reflects the evolution of the brand while staying true to its roots. From mountain trails to city streets, Victorinox ensures you're ready for wherever the journey leads.

• Victorinox, Rennweg 58, Zurich, victorinox.com

Recycle in Style

Rising from the industrial edges of Zurich-West, the *FREITAG Flagship Store Zurich* is a shop that doubles as a manifesto. Built from stacked shipping containers and reaching 85 feet, the tower sells unique bags made from recycled truck tarps, seat belts and inner tubes. Inside, the aesthetic is raw, the concept circular. Climb to the rooftop for sweeping views over railway lines and the evolving city, a fitting vantage point for a brand that turned waste into design and helped reshape the neighborhood around it. Two decades after opening its flagship, the sustainability stewards operate dozens of FREITAG stores around the world.

- **FREITAG Flagship, Geroldstrasse 17, Zurich, freitag.ch**

An Enduring Edge

Opened in Lucerne's Old Town in 1860, Weber's World has been the go-to place for Swiss Army knives since the start, five generations and counting. In fact, the photo was taken here in 1910. The small shop on Weinmarkt is now run by the couple Manuela and Pascal and feels more like a family tradition than a store. Visitors come for the huge selection of Swiss Army knives, pocketknives and kitchen blades, but also for the personal touch. Buy a knife and the team will engrave your name on the spot, free of charge. Many locals remember getting their first Swiss Army knife here as kids, making this historic shop one of Switzerland's most practical (and enduring) souvenir stops.

- **Weber's World, Weinmarkt 20, Lucerne, webers-world.com**

Photos: Claudio Biesele, Florian Bouvet-Fournier, Roland Tännler

Urban Arches

Under the railway arches in Zurich's creative District 5, IM VIADUKT is where locals shop, eat and hang out. Independent boutiques, design stores and food spots line the restored viaduct, with the lively Markthalle at its heart. Come for coffee and a croissant-like Gipfeli and browse homeware, fashion and Swiss-made goods. Then linger over oysters, schnitzel or dumplings. Many shopkeepers are the owners themselves, giving the place a friendly neighborhood feel. In summer, people spill into nearby parks. In winter, fondue gondolas and festive lights take over. It's less a mall than a slice of everyday Zurich life.

• IM VIADUKT, 8005, Zurich, im-viadukt.ch

Celestial Sync

The Chinese Calendar is a striking feat of horology, merging the Chinese lunisolar calendar with the Gregorian system. The watch, part of H. Moser & Cie's creative Endeavour line, tracks lunar months, zodiac signs and moon phases while remaining accurate for 12 years without adjustment. It represents a poetic bridge between ancient Eastern tradition and contemporary Swiss precision. Limited to just 100 pieces, the Chinese Calendar is currently available online by reservation, but it comes with a hefty price tag that tops six figures.

• Endeavour Chinese Calendar, h-moser.com/collections/endeavour

Photos: H. Moser & Cie

Nadja Stäubli

Life in Full Color

In 2012, photographer and creative director Nadja Stäubli set up *Sula* (sulaworld.com) in Zurich as a personal creative experiment. Years later, Sula has grown into one of the city's most distinctive design studios, specializing in rugs, textiles and objects. Blending traditional craftsmanship with cutting-edge production techniques, the brand has built a reputation on a bold, colorful aesthetic that feels both timeless and deeply rooted in contemporary culture. Collaborations with artists and designers sit at the heart of the studio's practice, keeping the work fresh and unexpected.

Sula began as a bachelor's thesis. How did it evolve into a brand?

The whole process evolved in a very organic way. For my bachelor's exhibition, I designed my first carpet, and the audience responded really well to it. Following that feedback, we produced a few more, just a very small number at the beginning. After that, we officially founded the company, and for the next two years, we worked very quietly, in rather run-down studio spaces here in Zurich. Gradually, as we launched new products, the label slowly started to grow. The friend I started the company with eventually left, so I hired an office administrator, and together we really developed Sula into a proper business.

Sula has a very distinct visual language: colorful, graphic and playful. How did that aesthetic evolve over time?

It came from a very intuitive place. Before Sula, I worked in photography and always had an instinct for color, without relying on theory or strict systems. That same approach carried into Sula. We didn't overthink things, and somehow it worked. I wanted the designs to feel timeless rather than overly trendy, and to stand apart from what already exists in this field. When you see our carpets in person, they're incredibly soft and very high quality. There really isn't much on the market that combines this woven, high-tech production with such graphic and colorful designs. I think it's that combination that gives Sula its very specific identity.

Collaborations seem to be an important part of Sula's work. How do you choose your partners, and what do you enjoy most about working with other designers and artisans?

Personally, I really enjoy working with specialists. For example, we recently did a small collaboration with a very well-known Swiss soap manufacturer. They created the soap, while I developed the scent, and together we designed a bath towel to accompany it as part of the set. Whether it's glass, lighting, perfume or something else, I love working with experts in their field.

Then there are collaborations that come from pure creative curiosity. Sometimes I see the work of an artist, illustrator or brand and immediately imagine how it could look translated into a woven piece. And of course, many projects also emerge naturally through

Museum für Gestaltung
Kreis 5

Cabaret Voltaire
Kreis 1

Rote Fabrik
Kreis 2

Schauspielhaus
Kreis 1 and 5

Pavillon Le Corbusier
Kreis 8

friendships and creative networks. You meet people, become friends, and at some point, someone says, "It would be great to create something together."

Rugs have a strong presence in a space. They shape the atmosphere of a room, and they also carry a long traditional history. That combination makes them a particularly exciting medium for many creatives.

How would you describe Zurich's design scene today, and where do you see Sula within it?

Zurich has a lot of pros and cons when it comes to the design scene. On one hand, it's a very small city, almost like a village, so the creative bubble is quite limited. At the same time, there are many talented people here. The challenge is that the broader landscape isn't built for creative industries. Many friends leave Zurich for cities like London, Paris, Berlin or New York, where opportunities in fashion, music and design are stronger. Switzerland leans toward finance, tech and healthcare, so design receives less structural support.

When it comes to the broader creative scene, which art spaces are a must?

The *Museum für Gestaltung* has an incredible collection of posters that is absolutely worth seeing if you're interested in Swiss graphic design. I'd also explore the galleries around Rämistrasse and the Löwenbräu Kunstareal, and visit *Cabaret Voltaire*—the birthplace of Dada—*Rote Fabrik*, *Schauspielhaus*, and the *Pavillon Le Corbusier*.

Volkshaus
Kreis 4

Hotel Kindli
Kreis 1

Ooki Pavillon
Kreis 5

Zum Guten Glück
Kreis 3

Silo Silo
Kreis 5

La Finestra
Kreis 1

Zentralwäscherei
Kreis 5

Widder Bar
Kreis 1

Heisswein
Kreis 5

Sacchi
Kreis 4

Schnupf
Kreis 4

Sula
Kreis 4

When you want to escape work and just enjoy Zurich, what does a day in the city look like for you?

In the summer, I love riding my bike around the city, going out for lunch or a cocktail and then heading to the river or the lake. Zurich is such a water city. The rivers and the lake are so clean and beautiful, and everyone is out enjoying them. At the lakes, there are these Badi spots, lakeside swimming areas with small cafés and bars, each with its own vibe.

What restaurants are your favorites?

I love *Volkshaus* for traditional Swiss dishes, *Kindli* for a more upscale traditional experience, *Ooki* for Japanese cuisine, *Zum Guten Glück* for pancakes and *Silo Silo* and *La Finestra* for casual dining. *Zentralwäscherei* is great for food, but also for the parties.

Which spots best capture the city's vibe after dark?

I love having a cosmopolitan at *Widder Bar. Heisswein* has great wine, *Sacchi Bar* is perfect for cocktails and people-watching and *Schnupf* is my go-to for late-night hangouts.

There are also lots of outdoor parties and "illegal" summer gatherings, which are really fun. This outdoor party scene is huge, mostly electronic music and techno raves, but also DJs playing dancehall, Caribbean, African and South American music. Everyone comes out and you get that small-city energy, which is really nice.

What do you think is a neighborhood worth exploring in Zurich, one that people might overlook?

My favorite is Kreis 3, where I live. It has that perfect mix of local life and hidden gems. I also recently rediscovered Kreis 1. It's traditionally a posh area near the Old Town and used to feel very touristy, but now I love strolling along the lake because it's really beautiful.

Zurich is surrounded by pristine nature, making it easy to get away for a few hours. Where do you usually go when you want a quick escape outdoors?

I really love taking the train from Zurich to Adliswil. From there, a gondola goes up the mountain, and you can walk for about two hours toward Uetliberg. It's a very easy walk, and along the way, there are grill stations where you can grab drinks or cake, and you can see the whole skyline of Zurich as you go.

There are also a lot of great hikes around Einsiedeln, about 30 to 40 minutes from the city, for ski tours. Another favorite is Graubünden, about an hour and a half from Zurich, for beautiful nature and amazing trails.

If I have more time, the Bernese Oberland is incredible. It's pristine nature with waterfalls, cows, flowers and wide-open mountain landscapes.

What do you think is the best season to visit Zurich?

Most definitely summer. You can just go from café to restaurant to bar, see all the people outside, everyone's in a good mood. You can go swimming or go dancing. People are happy and friendly, and the energy is completely different. It's like the city has a split personality in the summer.

Cinema Under the Stars

Each August, the lakeside town of Locarno turns into a cinephile's paradise during the *Locarno Film Festival*, one of Europe's most prestigious showcases for independent cinema. For more than 70 years, it has championed independent, experimental and boundary-pushing films, supporting emerging talents and great auteurs alike. Its most iconic setting is Piazza Grande, where thousands gather under the night sky for open-air screenings projected onto one of the world's largest screens. Set against the shimmering waters of Lake Maggiore and the surrounding mountains, the festival delivers a cinematic experience unlike any other.

• Locarno Film Festival, locarnofestival.ch

Gather

The Social Pulse

From world-class art fairs and open-air film festivals to jazz in the mountains and light trails through medieval streets, these are the events worth building a trip around.

Summit Sounds

Picture a storybook alpine village of wooden chalets, narrow streets and dramatic peaks rising in every direction. Each September, this remarkable setting hosts the *Zermatt Music Festival*, when leading orchestral musicians and young talents gather for concerts, master classes and rehearsals across the car-free mountain town. At the heart of the program is the Zermatt Festival Orchestra, whose players are drawn from top ensembles around the world. With the iconic Matterhorn towering above the village, the festival pairs world-class classical music with one of the most spectacular settings in the Alps.

• Zermatt Music Festival, zermattfestival.com

Photo: Festival del film Locarno

The Urban Canvas

The *Street Art Festival Frauenfeld* is a recent addition to Switzerland's urban art scene, but it's already leaving a visible mark on the city. Founded in 2023, each edition gathers around 70 international artists, transforming façades, riverbanks and even private homes into large-scale works. Projects range from socially engaged collaborations with local communities to striking commissions for historic houses, interactive murals and experimental pieces across public spaces. Over a summer weekend, Frauenfeld becomes a live studio, with workshops, music and guided tours, before settling into an open-air gallery that keeps the town buzzing long after.

• Street Art Festival Frauenfeld, www.isaff.ch

Carnival Fire

The Chienbäse in Liestal is one of Switzerland's most intense winter traditions. Held on the Sunday night before Fasnacht begins, the event sees locals shoulder fiery pinewood torches through the narrow Old Town streets. Towering wagons stacked with fire add to the spectacle, filling the air with heat and sparks. Rooted in centuries-old custom, this primal display of heat and sparks serves as a prelude to the hushed, lantern-lit Morgestraich that follows in nearby Basel.

• Chienbäse, Liestal, chienbaese.ch

Basel Art Takeover

For one week every June, the Swiss city of Basel becomes the center of the global art world. Since its founding in 1970, the *Art Basel* fair has grown into the most influential event in contemporary art, bringing together leading international galleries, collectors and industry professionals. Its pulse spills far beyond the halls of Messe Basel: Site-specific installations activate public spaces, satellite shows pop up across the city and underground parties run late into the night. Seeing Basel transform from its usual calm into a city buzzing with charged, cosmopolitan and slightly chaotic energy is an experience in itself.

• Art Basel, artbasel.com

Fashion Forward

Zurich joined the global fashion calendar in 2026 with the debut of *Zurich Fashion Week*, a multiday showcase of Swiss design, creativity and emerging talent. Held at the Kongresshaus, the event brings together established labels, rising designers and fashion students in a buzzy mix of runway shows, talks and industry gatherings. It builds on earlier local events such as Fashion Days, led by model and activist Tamy Glauser, but with a broader international outlook. Expect bold collections, fresh ideas and a glimpse into Switzerland's evolving fashion scene, proof that Zurich's creative side extends well beyond banking and chocolate.

• Zurich Fashion Week, zurichfashionweek.ch

Lucerne Lights Up

The historic city of Lucerne comes alive with contemporary light art during the *Lilu Light Festival Lucerne*, transforming winter darkness into wonder. Each January, artists from Switzerland and beyond illuminate squares, church façades, bridges and alleyways with more than 20 installations, from monumental projections to glowing sculptures, whimsical figures and immersive sound-and-light environments. Indoor concerts and live performances complement the installations, adding another layer to the experience. As darkness falls, visitors follow a trail of light through the cobbled streets of the medieval Old Town and along the lakeside, turning a winter stroll into a path of luminous discovery.

• Lilu Light Festival Lucerne, lichtfestivalluzern.ch

Vampire Jazz

Best known for its winter wonderland, St. Moritz reveals a different rhythm each summer during *Festival da Jazz*. International stars and rising talents gather for three weeks of concerts across the Engadin resort, with a festival celebrated for the rare intimacy it offers between artists and audiences. Open-air concerts fill parks, squares and lakeside stages, while many performances take place in the legendary *Dracula Club*, a tiny wood-paneled venue where audiences sit just a few feet from the stage. For extra fun, you can hunt for the Hidden Sessions with guerrilla-style secret gigs popping up at the last minute in unexpected spots.

• Festival da Jazz, St. Moritz, festivaldajazz.ch

Iced Polo

When polo meets snow, St. Moritz's frozen lake becomes a playground of elegance and adrenaline. The resort pioneered snow polo in 1985, hosting the world's first high-goal tournament on ice. Each winter, top players clash on the ice while a cosmopolitan crowd cheers from heated stands and lakeside terraces, champagne in hand, oysters on the side. Hooves thunder, mallets swing and snow flurries fly against a breathtaking mountain backdrop. Snow Polo delivers equal parts sporting thrill and social buzz, making it a one-of-a-kind winter spectacle.

• Snow Polo World Cup, St. Moritz, snowpolo-stmoritz.com

Run Wild

High-altitude miles meet alpine glamour at the annual *St. Moritz Running Festival,* held over three days in August among the crystalline lakes and peaks of the Engadin. The flagship event, *Engadiner Sommerlauf* (Engadin Summer Run), winds through forests and along lake shores for nearly 23 kilometers, making it slightly longer than a half-marathon. Other ways to experience the terrain include the 10.4km Run Pontresina through the postcard-perfect Val Roseg, the lake-hugging 6km Run S and the lung-busting 6.6km Free Fall Vertical up the legendary World Cup ski slope. Relay and kids' race round out the program, all within the polished St. Moritz backdrop.

• St. Moritz Running Festival, stmoritzrunningfestival.ch

Photos: Chris Czadilek, Giancarlo Cattaneo (fotoswiss.com) CC BY-SA 4.0, Henry Schulz

Showcase

The Zurich Underground

A photo showcase by Philipp Mueller

Zurich-born Philipp Mueller is a high-velocity photographer whose work spans fashion, sport and celebrity. He's shot global icons like Roger Federer and Ansel Elgort and brands such as Nike and Zenith, and his photos have appeared in publications including *L'Uomo Vogue, GQ* and *Vogue Germany*. But his visual language was forged far from the gloss of the mainstream. Mueller cut his teeth documenting punk, new wave and club scenes, a rawness captured in his book *120 BPM* and his upcoming follow-up (working title: *180 BPM*). Drawn from his archives, these photos document the Zurich underground across more than 40 years.

1980s

When I was 15, there was a club in Zurich called the Big Apple. The entrance to the club was an old English bus, and the owner was from the local chapter of the Hells Angels in Zurich. It was a wild mix of different youth cultures, from punks to psychobilly to skinheads. We were just naive 15-year-old kids. Through a friend, we found out about wearing black clothes and started to shave our heads on the side. I remember trying to put black *kohl* (eyeliner) on in the toilet at night. We didn't know. We came from the suburbs.

The club didn't serve alcohol, so that's how we got in as minors. We had to bring the alcohol ourselves. In the 1980s, no trains ran back to the suburbs, so we had to stay all night until five in the morning when the first trains would start running and people went to work.

The club closed after a year, so we went to other locations and started a little club ourselves with about 50 people. It was at a community center called Pink Teddy in the outskirts of Zurich. We spun The Cure and Depeche Mode, inspired by the Blitz club in London and Steve Strange from [the band] Visage. It was more like New Romantics, goth. At our last party, about 700 people came from everywhere.

1990s

Around 2015, I found all these forgotten pictures from the 1990s in my archive. Back in the day, I worked at a club and started taking photographs for local underground magazines. These are the photos in my published book *120 BPM*. At the time, a rave had to be a lot more creative, from bicycle tunnels, raves in the forest, basements and mountain fields to big raves in old factory halls.

Zurich nightlife at the end of the 1980s was a bit of a dead zone. It was all established, polished clubs, so some people started throwing small, illegal parties in Zurich's industrial zone. Doing a party with just a DJ in the center was boring, so we started doing fashion shows.

One club was raided by the police, but when they arrived, we just hid the panels with the pricing for the beverages. We told them it was a private party and that we weren't doing anything commercial, and they couldn't do anything. More and more people started doing this, and in the end, the police just gave up and let it be. That was the beginning of a very creative nightlife scene.

Today

For the new photo book, I thought it would be interesting to discover the scene as it is today, and I see the parallel to our new wave and punk scene. It's funny, they have parties that say "no phones or videos" on the flyer. These kids, they're like 18, 20, don't know a world before phones, but they say no for an evening because they want to enjoy each other and the music and only that. Last summer, I went to a big [commercial] rave, and it was completely different. Everyone had their phones in the air. They're not living the moment. They are keeping it to enjoy it later. I don't know, maybe it's just a different culture.

• philippmueller.co.uk

Art & Design

Creative Peaks

From a modernist church rising from avalanche rubble to massive biodegradable land art, this is a country that takes creativity seriously, in the most unexpected places.

Walk the Walls

Zurich's street art scene has an unlikely origin story. In the late 1970s, Harald Naegeli, the self-styled "Sprayer of Zurich," began covering the city's concrete façades with minimalist stick figures, sparking a cat-and-mouse game with police that made him famous worldwide. His works were once scrubbed off, but today they are protected heritage.

From those origins, the scene spread across the city, but it's in Zurich-West where it found its natural home, and where today it is most dense, most alive. This former industrial district is a layered, restless place where towering commissioned murals share walls with illegal tags and anonymous graffiti, the scene constantly shifting. In addition to his 3D *Sunny* (photo) in Wollishofen, REDL's monumental *Melody* on Limmatstrasse is one of the district's most recognizable works. One Truth Bros, whose lovable, sorrowful-eyed dogs have become one of Zurich's most beloved street art signatures, have left their own goofy, oversized canine on Hardturmstrasse. Nearby in Langstrasse, you'll find French artist C215's intimate stencil portraits, while Hardbrücke sports vivid color and strong lines from Oibel1. And keep an eye out for the Rüebli, a small carrot some anonymous artist has been leaving on walls across Zurich for years, with no one ever claiming responsibility.

The best way to take it all in is on foot, keeping your eyes on the walls and letting the district reveal itself. Start at Escher-Wyss-Platz, work through the factory district around *Im Viadukt* and *Geroldstrasse*, and end at *Frau Gerolds Garten* for drinks among shipping containers strung with fairy lights.

• Various Locations

Photo: Patrick REDL Wehrli

The Art Lab

Tucked inside Zurich's iconic Rote Fabrik, *Shedhalle* is a beloved artistic and social space that has championed experimental contemporary art for more than 40 years. A laboratory for creative exploration, the nonprofit venue presents site-specific installations, performances and collaborative projects that continually rethink how art is produced, presented and discussed. Its process-driven programs and socially engaged projects have pioneered inventive exhibition formats, influencing artists and institutions across Zurich and beyond. Blending experimentation, dialogue and community, Shedhalle remains a vital hub for the city's creative networks, offering a window into its cutting-edge art scene.

• Shedhalle, Seestrasse 395, Zürich, shedhalle.ch

Photos: Shedhalle, Foto Studio Pagi

The Lakeside Frame

At *MASI Lugano*, the view is almost part of the exhibition. The museum's main galleries stretch toward Lake Lugano, ending in vast windows that frame the mountains and water like a living backdrop. Sitting at the cultural crossroads between the north and south of the Alps, MASI presents a strong program of modern and contemporary art, pairing major international exhibitions with a deep engagement in Swiss and regional work. It's the perfect base to dive into cutting-edge art while taking in the landscapes and architecture of the Ticino region.

• MASI Lugano, Piazza Bernardino Luini 6, Lugano, masilugano.ch

The Stone Phoenix

In the tiny alpine village of Mogno is a surprising modernist gem: Mario Botta's *Church of San Giovanni Battista*. Rebuilt on the footprint of a 17th-century chapel destroyed by a 1986 avalanche, it preserves the original volume and two salvaged bells. Yet this modern masonry marvel is defined by its bold cylinder-and-rectangle form, clad in alternating stripes of white Peccia marble and gray Riveo granite that continue seamlessly inside. A glass roof floods the space with light, casting shifting patterns across the stone interior. Unexpectedly intimate, it remains one of Switzerland's most striking examples of contemporary sacred architecture.

• Church of San Giovanni Battista, 6696 Mogno, chiesadimogno.ch

Photos: Patrick Robert Doyle, Nicolas Quiniou

Mountain Soul

Housed in the century-old Villa Arona in St. Moritz-Dorf, the *Berry Museum* is a love letter to the Engadin. In this space, doctor-turned-artist Peter Robert Berry II, often described as the Van Gogh of the Alps, captured the healing silence of the mountains long before tourism reshaped the valley. His grandson, Dr. Peter Berry IV, established the museum to continue that legacy, exploring the intersection of art and wellness while preserving memories of a slower era of sleigh bells and snowbound passes. A visit feels like a visual detox, offering stillness and perspective amid the mountain landscape. Dr. Peter Berry IV also established the Zuort Lodge (zuort.ch), a place designed to experience the healing silence in person.

• Berry Museum, Via Arona 32, St. Moritz, berrymuseum.com

Land Art Legend

Swiss-French artist Saype is a pioneer of sustainable land art, world-renowned for his biodegradable frescoes painted directly onto the earth. Using a self-developed paint made from charcoal and chalk, he creates vast, ephemeral works like *Le terrain des Possibles* (above) in Geneva and *Bright Dreams* (below) at Zurich's Irchel Park. His meaningful works, which grace iconic locations from the Eiffel Tower to New York Harbor, are designed to fade naturally and leave no trace behind, except in galleries (right).

• Various locations

Pavillon Le Corbusier, Zurich

Art & Design

Cathedrals of Cool

Beyond the timber chalets and medieval spires lies a Switzerland forged in daring geometry and high-tech precision. From the quarter-million larch shingles of a bubble-shaped retreat to the elliptical galleries of a Zurich library, these landmarks epitomize the quiet coolness of modern Swiss design.

Zoo Zurich

Fiore di Pietra, Monte Generoso

Chesa Futura, St. Moritz

Law Library, University of Zurich

Messe Basel Pavilion

Rolex Learning Center, Lausanne

Photos: YueStock/Shutterstock.com, Basel Tourismus, Mihai-Bogdan Lazar/Shutterstock.com, pcdazero, Roland Fischer CC BY-SA 3.0, Walter Schärer CC BY 2.0, Andreas Buschmann.

Andreas Caminada

Inside the Castle Kitchen

Meet the man who turned Switzerland's smallest city into a global culinary destination. Andreas Caminada led *Schloss Schauenstein* to three Michelin stars, becoming one of the youngest chefs to reach the industry's highest level. He later earned a star for his garden-driven *Oz* and has mentored a new generation of star-winning chefs. Despite it all, he remains a mountain man at heart, pairing exacting technique with a deep connection to his Graubünden roots.

Schloss Schauenstein
Fürstenau

Oz
Fürstenau

Golf Club Patriziale Ascona
Ascona

Golf Club Lugano
Magliaso

Golf Club Alvaneu Bad
Alvaneu Bad

Buna Vista Golf Sagogn
Sagogn

Golf Club Bad Ragaz
Bad Ragaz

Technique is key, but in places like Switzerland, the story is also in the sourcing. What are examples of seasonality in the menu?

We maintain a private garden to stay strictly seasonal. Our cellar is filled with ferments and pickles through the winter, but the menu shifts to green as soon as spring hits. We just harvested our first leaves and have been experimenting with cabbage, including red cabbage ice cream. It's a refreshing starter that relies on acidity and contrast. In April, the asparagus arrives alongside the wild garlic we harvest from the forest below the castle. In the summer, the garden transforms again, making way for bok choy, broccoli and carrots. Every season has its own color. Our dishes are a direct reflection of what is happening in the garden.

You were a pastry chef early in your career. What did you learn from pastry that proved to be beneficial in creating savory dishes?

It's all about the precision, the way you handle products and the way you plate. I loved working with chocolate and creating those very thin, delicate decorations. It requires incredibly precise work, and you can see that influence in my dishes today. Being in pastry was a big part of my development, allowing me to transfer this approach to the savory side. I now try to push my chefs to spend time in pastry, even if they're afraid of it or claim they don't like it. I tell them it's essential because it forces you to work with a higher level of accuracy.

You spent time in Vancouver kitchens. What did you learn about other global flavors that you applied to Swiss menus?

I grew up in the mountains just 20 minutes from here, raised on traditional food based on potatoes and flour. Vancouver was a big eye-opener for me. While I was there for English school, a friend helped me land a job at a golf course restaurant in Horseshoe Bay. More importantly, he managed to get me one-day placements at top restaurants like Rob Feenie's *Le Crocodile* and *Lumière*. Those days influenced my career immensely. They showed me just how diverse and precise global cuisine could be. Vancouver was also where I learned to play golf.

Where's the best place in Switzerland to golf?

There are so many, but if you're in the south of Switzerland, *Ascona* and *Lugano* are both beautiful. Closer to our place, we have three great courses. One is *Alvaneu Bad*, which is more of a mountain course. There is *Sagogn*, which is in the village where I grew up. They opened a beautiful course there about 15 years ago. Then we have *Bad Ragaz*, which is a fantastic place that has been around for

Photo: Caminada Group

Casa Casutt
Ilanz

Mulania
Laax

Riva Grisuna
Sagogn

more than a century. I try to play all of them once in a while.

You loved snowboarding in your 20s. Do you still snowboard?

Yes, it was a huge passion. Even when I was in Vancouver, I made sure to go up to Whistler a few times. As my career as a chef grew, I didn't have much time, but I always managed to get on the slopes at least once a year. Now that my kids are 10 and 12, I've started skiing again as well. This year, I managed five days of skiing and snowboarding. It's not enough, but I'm still happy I can do it.

What are your favorite slopes in Switzerland?

I grew up in Sagogn, which is right next to Laax. It's a fantastic ski resort, and we love to go there with the kids. The slopes are great, the snow is reliable and it's only 20 minutes away from us. It is still my favorite.

What's your favorite restaurant in Laax?

There are a few. One is in a nearby village, Ilanz, called *Casa Casutt*. It's a great place with an amazing chef. I always go there for the tartare with Rösti. It's a typical rösti, but very crispy. There is another one called *Mulania*, located right before you head up the mountain. The owner is very nice, and it's a beautiful spot to visit.

Where do you go for comfort food, and what kind of comfort food do you like?

For traditional comfort food, there is *Riva Grisuna*. The chef there is amazing and has been running the restaurant for many years. She makes a traditional pear ravioli from the region, filled with dried pears and served with brown butter and salsiccia sausage. It's a savory dish, but with that sweetness from the fruit. It is very hard to get a table there, you need "vitamin B" (connections) because everyone wants to go there. It's beautiful. I also love Capuns, which is another traditional dish for this region.

What can diners do to make the most of their culinary experience at one of your restaurants?

We have rooms here at the castle, which is located in Fürstenau, the smallest city in the world. It's a historical place. The town is beautiful, and you can take a bike up to Canovasee, which is a lovely lake for a summer swim. Nearby, we have the Viamala, a dramatic, historical route with deep gorges that feel like a cave. We are just 15 minutes from Chur, the capital of the region, which has a beautiful art museum and great pastry shops. Then there is Flims Laax, where you'll find Caumasee. It's a stunning lake in the middle of the forest that looks a bit like the Caribbean. We even have the Ruinaulta, the "Grand Canyon of Switzerland," only 15 minutes away.

You're famous for cooking from the garden, but how would you describe your approach to proteins like steak, fish and chicken?

I've never been a fan of heavy sides like rice or potatoes in a tasting menu. We love vegetables, but of course, you need protein. We use local fish like pike-perch, whitefish and *omble chevalier* (Arctic char), which is in the trout family. We have incredible local meats and chicken available to us. Our menu usually starts with four vegetable-driven snacks from the garden, followed by a cold, fresh fish dish. Later, we might serve sweetbreads, quail or another fish course. For

the main course, we always feature a piece of meat that reflects the season. Right now, we have lamb on the menu. In the summer, we love working with pork and barbecue flavors. As we move into fall, we transition to wild game like deer and chamois. Every season brings its own perfect meat, and we love integrating those variations.

Space Copenhagen recently helped renovate the castle. What kind of renovations did you do?

We opened the restaurant with four rooms back in 2003. Over the next 20 years, we made many changes, but eventually, we felt the house had lost its "red line" (or common theme). The design had become a bit of a mix. We decided to return to the castle's essence. Working with Space Copenhagen, we focused on using local materials to highlight the building's natural beauty, adding timeless furniture and personal art to keep it cozy. It's now reduced to the max, yet still very personal. In a way, the architecture has developed just like our cuisine. It feels like it always did, yet it's completely different and modern.

Who are your favorite Swiss designers working in the restaurant industry?

I work closely with Stefano Triacca. He is fantastic when it comes to industrial design and specialized items. There are great studios like Atelier Oï that are internationally famous for their work with major brands and luxury hotels. I recently met the owner, and we hope to collaborate soon. Switzerland has so many icons. We have designers like Trix and Robert Haussmann, and world-class architects like Peter Zumthor and Valerio Olgiati. For historical projects, we often work with Gasser Derungs. They are excellent at modernizing heritage spaces.

What other projects do you have in the works?

We are currently busy with renovations at the castle and expanding our garden projects, but the real goal isn't just to open new places. Opening a restaurant is the easy part. The challenge is maintaining the quality and helping those projects evolve over time. That takes a lot of work, but I enjoy staying on top of it and keeping everything updated.

Riverside Grotto

Tucked beside the Maggia River in Ponte Brolla, *Grotto America* is a classic Ticino grotto with real staying power. Dating back to the 1800s, it's long been a meeting place, and it still feels that way. Expect stone tables under chestnut trees, a breezy riverside terrace and a menu rooted in local tradition, from cured meats and alpine cheeses to seasonal, home-style dishes. In summer, things pick up with live music and art evenings, but the essence stays the same: unfussy food, local wine and a setting made for whiling away the hours.

• Grotto America, Via ai Grotti 71, Ponte Brolla, grottoamerica.ch

Bites

Tables with a View

From cliff-clinging dining rooms to glass-wrapped domes, Swiss restaurants take the idea of a great view and elevate it. You might hike through caves or ride a cable car to get there, but the setting doesn't just frame the meal: It often shapes it.

Glass & Gruyère

One of the six restaurants at *AlpenGold Hotel* in Davos, the *Cheese Factory* is a glass-wrapped spot dedicated entirely to Switzerland's favorite ingredient. Think fondue, raclette and other cheese-heavy classics served in a slick, alpine setting that feels equal parts cozy and contemporary. It's unapologetically indulgent, the kind of place you come to lean into melted everything after a day in the mountains. Come hungry, settle in and work your way through bubbling pots and golden layers, ideally with a glass of something crisp on the side.

• Cheese Factory, Baslerstrasse 9, Davos, alpengoldhotel.com

Terrace in the Sky

For stratospheric views of the Imperial Crown at 9,000 feet, *Espace Weisshorn* delivers high-altitude dining with serious style. Set at the top of the Zinal–Sorebois gondola and Grimentz cable car, it's a ski-in (or hike-in) spot with a strong focus on sustainability and regional sourcing. Expect alpine flavors reworked with a modern touch: house-made preserves from wild berries, mountain herbs and carefully selected local produce. The real showstopper, though, is the terrace, a sweeping panorama of peaks that feels almost unreal, stretching across some of the highest mountains in the Alps.

• Espace Weisshorn, Sorebois Summit, Zinal, Val d'Anniviers, espaceweisshorn.ch

Culinary Cliffhanger

Clinging dramatically to a cliff in the Alpstein mountains, *Berggasthaus Aescher* is less about what's on the plate—though you'll find highly satisfying alpine classics such as creamy barley soup, buttermilk bramata and meatloaf with potatoes—and more about where you're eating it. Built into the rock face above the valley, it's one of Switzerland's most photographed spots, and for good reason. Getting here is part of the experience. Take the Ebenalp cable car from Wasserauen, then walk 15 minutes through the Wildkirchli caves or hike up via Seealpsee. Either way, arrive hungry and stay for the view.

• Berggasthaus Aescher, Schwende-Rüte, aescher.ch

Photos: Luca Crivelli, Miranda Ajdini, AlpenGold Hotel Davos

Lindt
HOME OF CHOCOLATE

The Art of Chocolate

In Kilchberg, a quaint municipality just south of Zurich, *the Lindt Home of Chocolate* is a full-scale immersion into Switzerland's most famous export. Home to the largest Swiss chocolate museum, it traces the story of Swiss chocolate from bean to bar, charting the innovations and craftsmanship that shaped the historic Swiss chocolate. Interactive exhibits sit alongside archival material and contemporary design, making it as engaging for first-timers as it is for devoted chocophiles.

Besides the cocoa, the architecture alone is worth the trip. A sweeping, light-filled atrium forms the heart of the building, where the world's tallest free-standing chocolate fountain rises in a gleaming column of flowing chocolate. Standing 30 feet tall and featuring 370 gallons of real chocolate cascading at a rate of 2.2 pounds per second, it's a showstopping centerpiece and an unmistakable photo moment, but also a reflection of the scale and ambition of the space. Clean lines, warm tones and expansive curves give the interior a contemporary, welcoming feel, balancing wow factor with Swiss precision.

Beyond the museum galleries, the complex houses the largest Lindt boutique in the world, a treasure trove for gifting and discovery, as well as the first Lindt Café in Switzerland. Here, cocoa takes on new forms, from refined pastries to the brand's iconic hot chocolate, all of which are rich, comforting and especially welcome in the cooler months.

Seasonal touches add another dimension. In winter, a Choco Chalet stands outside the building, serving hot chocolate and mulled wine against a backdrop of twinkling fairy lights, decorated trees and festive music. The atmosphere is magical, transforming the forecourt into a cozy alpine scene. Special events during Christmas and Easter bring further celebration, making it a destination that evolves with the calendar.

For those keen to go beyond observation, chocolate courses at the Lindt CHOCOLATERIA, led by Lindt Master Chocolatiers, provide a hands-on perspective. Seasonal workshops run throughout the year, offering insight into techniques and flavor combinations, and teaching students how to make anything from chocolate bars to pralines.

Before you leave, a secret tip: At the tasting stations, try all three chocolate fountains on one spoon for a layered swirl of textures and intensities. It's a small ritual that neatly sums up the place. Just be sure to book tickets in advance for one of Switzerland's most distinctive culinary experiences.

• Lindt Home of Chocolate, Schokoladenplatz 1, Kilchberg, lindt-home-of-chocolate.ch

Photo: Fidel Fernando

The Cheese Atlas

More than just a product, Swiss cheese feels like a landscape translated into flavor. Local herbs, glacier water, altitude and centuries-old technique all leave their mark, creating wheels that taste unmistakably Swiss. While classics like Emmental AOP and Le Gruyère AOP are known around the world, they represent only a fraction of the country's diversity. Beyond these famous exports, Switzerland is home to more than 700 varieties of cheese, many being regional specialties produced in small batches and closely tied to seasonality.

Strict AOP (Appellation d'Origine Protégée) standards govern much of the production, dictating everything from the feed (fresh grass in summer, hay in winter) to the milk in general. Raw milk is typically the starting point, gently heated in copper vats. To taste something exceptional, start here:

Sbrinz AOP—One of Europe's oldest cheeses and the Swiss answer to Parmigiano, only nuttier, drier and often shaved or broken into shards rather than grated.

L'Etivaz AOP—A rare summer cheese made in copper cauldrons over open flames high in the Vaud Alps. Complex, slightly smoky and deeply tied to alpine pasture.

Vacherin Mont-d'Or AOP—Winter indulgence from the Jura. Warm it, and the interior collapses into a spoonable, woodsy, almost decadent cream.

Appenzeller AOP—The mysterious herbal brine, with each wheel regularly rubbed by hand, makes this one of the most flavorsome cheeses in Switzerland.

Tête de Moine AOP—Literally "monk's head," traditionally shaved into delicate rosettes. The texture is airy, the flavor nutty and floral.

Formaggio d'Alpe Ticinese AOP—Raw-milk cheeses from the Italian-speaking south of the country that tend to be more rustic and shaped by chestnut forests and warmer climates.

Decentralized cheesemaking is the norm, with small businesses producing almost two-thirds of the cheese. For a traditional Swiss experience, check out the Chästeilet ritual in the Justistal valley. After a summer of communal grazing, herders descend from the high pastures and stack their wheels into towering piles. The cheese is then divided among farmers according to how much milk their cows produced, a centuries-old ceremony that feels as much about community as it does about cheese.

Which are the best producers? Experts weigh in every two years at the Swiss Cheese Awards, where around 200 judges evaluate roughly 1,000 cheeses from across the country. The 2024 winners ranged from a standout Gruyère AOP by Fromagerie de Lanthen to an exceptional Vacherin Mont-d'Or AOP from Fromagerie André SA, proof that excellence here stretches from iconic classics to regional gems.

Inside the World of Stefan Wiesner
Cooking
with Nature

In a UNESCO-listed landscape with forest and moor areas in Central Switzerland, chef Stefan Wiesner has created a cuisine that cannot be easily defined. Known as "The Sorcerer of Entlebuch," Wiesner cooks with what most chefs would overlook, like wild plants, moss, bark, charcoal, ash, stones, even rusty iron, and transforms them over a wood fire into dishes that evoke the smell and texture of the landscape. At *Wiesner Mysterion* in Barmboden (Romoos)—his Michelin- and Green-starred, 18-point Gault&Millau restaurant—meals are conceived as sensory journeys shaped by foraging, storytelling and a philosophy that draws as much from art and science as from cooking itself.

You're known as both a chef and a naturalist. How do you define your relationship with nature?

I simply started cooking regional and seasonal food. But over time, I realized that nature offers much more than just ingredients. I work with everything: trees, stones, soil, plants and animals. From nose to tail and from root to leaf, nothing is excluded. Nature is a complete system, and I try to understand it and cook with it.

What do you look for when you go out to forage?

Sometimes I look for something specific, but often it's the opposite—something finds me. It can be an aroma, a texture, a feeling. If something interests me, I develop it further. It's not just about what you can eat. It's about what you can transform.

Your dishes are often described as tasting like nature itself. How do you translate a landscape into something edible?

It's about meaning. When I cook with a stone, it's not because I want to serve a stone. It's about its minerals, its temperature, its memory. We work with ash, peat, wood, plants, animals, even metal. These elements create depth. They allow us to express a place.

Your menus are inspired by art, music and philosophy. How does a dish begin for you?

Every menu has a theme. My cooking has been inspired by artists like Joseph Beuys, movements like Dada or Futurism, composers such as Alexander Nicolai and Fazıl Say, literature, Paracelsus, the elements and the planets. I've even created menus based on personal experiences, such as illness, childhood or my vintage car. I take the theme and ask: Where does it come from? What does it feel like? What textures and aromas does it have? Then I translate that into food, into chords.

So a menu becomes a kind of narrative?

Yes. Because I can cook with everything, I can tell stories. A menu is not just a meal but an expression of an idea that becomes an experience and evokes emotions.

You think about cooking in terms of "chords," almost like music. What does that mean in practice?

Cooking is like music. You have textures, aromas, temperatures, and when you combine them, you create chords. A single element is simple. But when you combine elements, the dish becomes more complex and more interesting. That's where cooking really begins.

Can you give an example?

You can take an ingredient like a carrot with its greens and use every part of it in different ways: raw, cooked, fried, converted, pickled, fermented, extracted, distilled, dried, turned into oil, even into charcoal and ash. It's still the carrot but expressed differently. Together, they become much more

Photos: Olivia Pulver

powerful than a single preparation. I call this monotypic cooking and spagyric cooking.

You have created visual maps of your approach, connecting botany, chemistry and philosophy. Why was it important to formalize this?

Because cooking is knowledge. We work with plants, water, minerals, animals, but also with perception, memory and emotion. If you understand how these interact, you can cook on a deeper level.

Food seems closely connected to memory for you, almost like music. How do you see this connection?

Yes. That's neurogastronomy. A dish can take you back in time. For example, if I cook your mother's potato salad, you become the little boy or girl you once were. If you hear a song linked to an old love, you are automatically transported back to that time. We can work with this to change perception and create emotional connections.

Even something as simple as water plays a role in cooking.

Of course. When I visit a big city and I have to brush my teeth with mineral water because the tap water is full of chlorine, I always wonder: What water are the chefs cooking with? Understanding water is where cooking begins. We have rainwater, snow water, spring and mineral water, groundwater, stream water, river water, lake water and seawater. Each type of water is different and changes the dish. Most people don't think about it, but this is where cooking starts.

There is something almost alchemical about your approach to cooking. Do you see it that way?

Yes, it's about transformation. We change textures, aromas and perception. We work with physical and sensory processes. That's where the real work—the cooking—lies.

This is a different approach from traditional fine dining. Was that a challenge?

Yes. I am a bit of an outsider. Many chefs focus on luxury ingredients like caviar, foie gras and wagyu. But for me, what matters is what surrounds us. Not everyone understands this, but that's okay.

After all these years, what still surprises you about nature?

It is not nature that is never complete but humanity. Nature shows us something new every day, and we are allowed to share and improve our knowledge. According to the motto: love, wisdom and strength.

Available from LOST iN

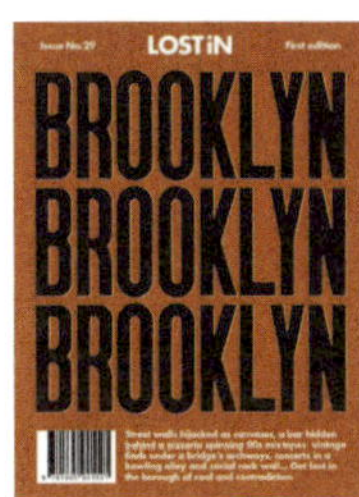

Shop the City Guides at www.lostin.com

@lostincityguides
@lost_in_travel

Raised Glasses

From wine tastings on a boat to vinyl-spun cocktail bars and castle cellar ghosts, Switzerland's drinking culture is as varied as its landscapes. Sip local, stay awhile and make the most of your pour decisions.

The Haunted Pour

Just minutes from *Château de Chillon*, UNESCO-listed vineyards spill toward the shores of Lake Geneva, producing a Grand Cru (Clos de Chillon) that's aged in the castle's medieval cellars. Only around 10,000 bottles are made each year, poured and sold exclusively on-site. But it might not be the cold Chasselas that's giving you the chills. A dark past has long fed rumors of hauntings, and each October, the castle leans into the legend with candlelit halls and its annual Scary Night event.

• Chillon Castle, Avenue de Chillon 21, Veytaux, chillon.ch

The Listening Shrine

In the slightly unhinged heart of Zurich Langstrasse, *Kasheme* is less a bar and more a gentle intervention for your listening habits. Part record store, part cocktail shrine, it feels like you've stumbled into the impeccably curated living room of someone whose vinyl collection costs more than your rent. Vintage furniture and warm amber lighting set the stage for a curated sonic journey through jazz, soul and world rhythms. By day, you can flip through records like a crate-digging purist. By night, things loosen up with Selector's Choice sessions and a basement mini-club. Kasheme isn't trying to be the loudest spot on the street, just the coolest.

• Kasheme, Neugasse 56, Zurich, kasheme.com

The Floating Cellar

Each autumn, *Expovina Wine Ships* turns Lake Zurich into a floating wine fair, with a fleet of moored boats transformed into tasting rooms. Wander from deck to deck sampling wines from Switzerland and beyond, chatting with producers and discovering new favorites along the way. The experience is very relaxed and highly social, which makes it one of the best ways to sip wine, really. Go at sunset for the best atmosphere, when the lake reflects the city lights and the whole thing feels quietly festive.

• Expovina Wine Ships, Bürkliplatz, Lake Zurich, expovina.ch

Bear Park Brew

Located at the foot of an actual bear park, *Altes Tramdepot* pours pints brewed on-site inside a former tram depot. Massive copper vats serve as centerpieces within the industrial-chic space, but let's be honest: You're here for the terrace. The outdoor seating spills out toward a panoramic view of storybook Old Town rooftops and the winding loops of the Aare River. The house beers range from clean, crushable classics to seasonal curveballs, all engineered for lazy sessions that blur into early evening. Pair your drink with something unapologetically Swiss, settle in and watch the light shift over the river like it's part of the service. If you leave after one pint, you're either disciplined or simply doing Bern wrong.

• Altes Tramdepot, Grosser Muristalden 6, Bern, altestramdepot.ch

Photos: Mathyas Kurmann, Giles Laurent CC BY-SA 4.0

Chandra Kurt

Decoding Swiss Wine

Switzerland's wine scene is a study in contrasts, shaped by steep terraces, four national languages and a wealth of indigenous grapes found nowhere else on earth. Chandra Kurt, one of the country's leading voices on wine, has spent decades decoding this quietly exceptional landscape, authoring more than 20 books along the way. From the sun-drenched slopes of the Valais to standout supermarket bottles under 30 CHF, she shares her insider guide to drinking like a local in the heart of the Alps.

For someone new to Swiss wine, what are the top three grapes they should try first?

Swiss wine has an extraordinary diversity of grape varieties and a large number of indigenous grapes rarely found in other countries. The two main grapes are Pinot Noir for the reds and Chasselas for the whites, and for indigenous, I would go for Petite Arvine.

Pinot Noir is cultivated in most of the country, and you can compare the influence of climate and winemaking traditions in the wines. My favorites are from Graubünden in German-speaking Switzerland or the Neuchâtel area.

Chasselas is a table grape for most countries, but in Switzerland, it's the star of Lake Geneva. Most of the wines are not labeled as Chasselas, but with the names of the villages they are from, such as Aigle, St. Saphorin or Féchy, a similar system to Burgundy. The most complex Chasselas can be found in the UNESCO-protected area of the Lavaux with the historic terroirs of Dézaley or Calamin.

Then there is the Petite Arvine grape. It seduces with a rich aromatic profile of honey, peach compote, tangerine essence and a touch of sweet-sour notes. A true Swiss ambassador of alpine wine culture.

You've collaborated with vineyards to produce wines that specialize in indigenous varieties like Chasselas and Cornalin. What are your favorite characteristics of the indigenous grapes?

The aromatic storytelling can be a surprise when you taste a specific grape for the first time. You discover how multifaceted the language of grapes is. It's like notes that create different melodies. You can also discover the expression of the soil and climate through a specific grape that only thrives in a limited zone. Especially with historic indigenous grapes, you learn the evolution of the taste of wine.

Among the six main wine regions, which offers the best price-to-quality ratio?

This is not easy to say as each region has a different grape portfolio. Labor in Switzerland is not cheap, and the landscape is marked by hills, making the work more intensive. I often hear that Swiss wine is expensive. I would not really agree, but I would say it is not cheap. We don't have the landscape to produce very cheap wines. But if you compare what a basic Burgundy costs to a Swiss wine, we are very reasonable. If you spend 15 to 20 CHF for a bottle, you get a magic wine. And most of the very high-end wines are less than 50 CHF.

Which wine region is best for vineyard tours and tastings?

I would start in the region of Vaud at the shores of Lake Geneva. It's a breathtaking landscape with the lake, vineyards and mountains. You could make a base in the village of Cully at *Auberge du Raisin* and plan trips to wine producers from there. Visiting the Dézaley terroir is a must, and you can also try to walk on the very steep slopes. It teaches you the hard work of wine growing.

Bündner Herrschaft is a very beautiful area with the wine villages of Fläsch, Maienfeld, Jenins and Malans. The center is Maienfeld. Here, at the gateway to Graubünden, Johanna Spyri wrote her bestselling children's book, *Heidi*. In this wine-growing region, you'll find well-known wine families such as the Gantenbeins, Donatschs, Fromms, Adanks, Davazs, Obrechts, Studachs and Wegelins.

The restaurant *Alter Torkel* in Jenins is a must, and a very good hotel with reasonable prices is the *Hotel Rössli* in Bad Ragaz. In the Valais region, there are two unique hiking experiences in the vineyards. The famous Heida trail in Visperterminen leads to one of the highest vineyards in Europe. The other is from the wine museum in Salgesch to the wine museum in Sierre.

If ordering Swiss wine at a restaurant, are there any AOC designations that diners should gravitate toward?

Every region has regulations of its own, and there are 63 AOCs at the moment, which may be a place name, a combination of place and grape name, or a generic name. Personally, I just try to enjoy the local wine of the place I visit.

Photo: Olivia Pulver

Auberge de Raisin
Cully

Alter Torkel
Jenins

Hotel Rössli
Bad Ragaz

St. Jodern Kellerei
Visperterminen

Any tips for food and wine pairings in Switzerland?

Our famous combination of the Chasselas wine Fendant and raclette or fondue. And then perch fillet from the lake of Geneva with a Chasselas or a lightly chilled Pinot Noir. A complex Merlot from Ticino is also very beautiful with steaks from Swiss cows. Or a capuns, a Swiss dumpling from Graubünden with a Pinot Noir or a Chardonnay from the region.

Weinseller Journal evaluates supermarket wines. What is your best tip for finding a hidden gem on a Swiss grocery shelf without spending more than 20 to 30 CHF?

Coop: Heida Cooperation Wine, Provins; Fendant Grand Cru Balavaud, Domaine Jean-René Germanier; Œil de Perdrix Rosé, Château d'Auvernier.

Denner: La Tour de Chata, Mont-sur-Rolle.

Volg: Riesling-Silvaner Goldbeere, Rutishauser DiVino; Merlot Ticino, Selezione d'Autore.

If someone wants to splurge on a Grand Cru, what would be your top pick?

I'd go to the region of Valais where you have Grand Cru appellations for indigenous grapes. You could focus on the Petite Arvine grape, and there are Grand Crus from Sierre, Chamoson, Saillon and Fully.

What emerging region and grape do you think will be the next star of the Swiss wine scene?

The main grapes are Pinot Noir and Chasselas, followed by Merlot, Gamay, Gamaret and Garanoir for the reds and Müller-Thurgau, Chardonnay, Silvaner and Petite Arvine for the whites. There are around 250 grape varieties cultivated in the country in total, 55 percent red and 45 percent white. What is growing more and more are fungus-resistant varieties known as PIWIs. So far, they are more known in the Swiss-German part, but other regions are planting them, too.

You've authored 20 books. Do you have a new title in the works?

Werd Verlag just published my newest book, *High-Altitude Vineyards*. More than 25 years ago, the Swiss wine pioneer and visionary Donald Hess went to Argentina and created a winery at 3,100 meters (about 10,000 feet) above sea level. It was the highest in the world at that time. To honor his legacy, we collaborated with talented wine writers from all over the world to explore other high-altitude vineyards to get a glimpse into this part of the wine world. We feature wineries from 11 different countries: Argentina, Bolivia, Chile, China, Cyprus, France, Italy, Peru, Spain, Switzerland and the USA. I orchestrated the book and also wrote a chapter about the *St. Jodern Kellerei* in Visperterminen.

You wrote a book about whisky and food. What are the keys to creating an optimal pairing?

It's similar to wine, but whisky plays a bigger role in providing additional taste, like a spice for food. I always think it's safest to combine the same with the same, like the smoky aromas of an Islay whisky with a steak from the fire with smoky notes. Or a lighter Highland whisky with poultry and a creamy sauce that can also contain a dash of this whisky. Of course, very important, the perfect match simply doesn't exist. There are many, and it's important to approach this topic with a relaxed and curious attitude. Otherwise, it will become a real ordeal.

Take your time.
In every time zone.

Fly nonstop to Switzerland.

STAR ALLIANCE

Swiss all the way.

Culture

The Reel Bucket List

Switzerland may be small, but its impact on film and music is anything but. From Bond chases to rock anthems, this is where icons came to create, escape and leave a mark. Now it's your turn to step into the frame.

The Villain's Lair

James Bond has chased, jumped and crashed through the Swiss landscapes since Sean Connery's iconic *Goldfinger* chase on the Furka Pass, but few places let you live out a Bond fantasy quite like *Piz Gloria*. The revolving mountaintop restaurant is the space Blofeld called home in *On Her Majesty's Secret Service*. The production team helped finance its completion in exchange for using it as the villain's alpine lair, one of cinema's most glamorous building deals. Today, the *Spy World* exhibition keeps the mythology alive, while the restaurant slowly turns to reveal the Eiger, Mönch, Jungfrau and 200 other peaks.

• Piz Gloria, Mürren, schilthorn.ch

Aliens in the Alps

H. R. Giger spent a career blending flesh and machine into a nightmarish, biomechanical universe, equal parts terrifying and beautiful. When Ridley Scott stumbled upon his art book *Necronomicon*, it led to Giger designing the entire visual universe of *Alien*, including the creature that has haunted cinema ever since. After falling in love with Gruyères, a medieval town better known for cheese, the Swiss artist bought a 13th-century château and turned it into his museum, spanning six decades of paintings, sculptures and film designs. Next door, his bar, with every surface molded in bone and biomechanical forms, is an experience unto itself.

• H. R. Giger Museum, Rue du Château 2, Gruyères, hrgigermuseum.com

Photos: Andy Davies ©HRGigerMuseum, fatmagulb/Shutterstock.com

Bollywood Romance

Switzerland is one of Bollywood's most beloved settings. Indian filmmakers have been shooting romantic song-and-dance sequences here since the 1960s, but it was director Yash Chopra who made it iconic. Discovering the Interlaken region in 1970, he kept returning, turning its meadows, lakes and snowy peaks into a visual shorthand for love. His most beloved film, *Dilwale Dulhania Le Jayenge*, transformed the village of Saanen and the bridge at Montbovon (photo) into pilgrimage sites for Indian tourists. Switzerland took note, honoring Chopra with a bronze statue in Interlaken.

• Interlaken, madeinbern.com

Gstaad's Leading Lady

Few visitors have left a mark on Gstaad quite like Hollywood icon Julie Andrews. The *Mary Poppins* and *Sound of Music* star first fell for the village in 1968, calling it "love at first sight," and bought a chalet three years later. In the 1970s, struck by how the village's charming rooftops disappeared into darkness each winter night, she purchased 1,000 Christmas lights and funded their upkeep for a decade. The so-called Julie-Lämpli still twinkles along the Hauptstrasse today. In 2014, Gstaad made it official, awarding Andrews honorary citizenship of Saanen, granted only 10 times.

• Gstaad, gstaad.ch

Sherlock's Last Stand

In 1893, Arthur Conan Doyle killed off Sherlock Holmes and chose Switzerland to do it. So struck by the wildness of the Reichenbach Falls near Meiringen, he set the final showdown between Holmes and Professor Moriarty in *The Final Problem* at the edge of its thundering 400-foot drop, with both men plunging to their deaths. The outcry from readers was so fierce that Doyle eventually brought Holmes back. The waterfall has made appearances in the 2011 film *Sherlock Holmes: A Game of Shadows* and in the BBC series *Sherlock*. Today, a cable car takes visitors to the very platform where the duel took place. A Sherlock Holmes museum sits in the town below.

• Reichenbach Falls, Meiringen

Eastwood's Edge

Over decades, the Eiger's North Face claimed some of climbing's finest lives, rightfully earning its nickname *Mordwand*, or "Murder Wall." In 1975, Clint Eastwood took on the 6,000-foot face for *The Eiger Sanction*, doing his own stunts where most actors would never dare. He cut his own rope and dangled freely in space above a thousand-foot drop, then ordered a repeat take just to make sure. Today, the Jungfrau railway delivers visitors to the heart of the Bernese Alps, with viewpoints that put the legendary North Face in full, frightening perspective.

• Eiger's North Face, Grindelwald

The Alderaan Archive

Grindelwald's mountains have stood in for many things, but a galaxy far, far away might be the most unexpected. For *Star Wars: Episode III—Revenge of the Sith*, George Lucas sent crews to capture plate photography of the jagged, snow-capped peaks around the Eiger, which were then combined with studio footage to create Alderaan, Princess Leia's home planet. No actors, no cameras rolling on location, just the mountains doing what they do best: looking impossibly cinematic.

• Grindelwald, grindelwald.swiss

Photos: Patrick Robert Doyle, Terra3 CC BY-SA 3.0

Rock Star Retreat

Music history runs deep on the Swiss Riviera. In particular, Montreux drew legends like the Rolling Stones, Lady Gaga, AC/DC and Shania Twain to its recording studios. Queen and David Bowie's "Under Pressure"? Recorded here. Deep Purple's "Smoke on the Water"? Written and recorded here after the band saw the *Montreux Casino* go up in flames during a Frank Zappa show. Adding to the prestige, Miles Davis and Nina Simone are just a few of the icons who took the stage at the *Montreux Jazz Festival* since its founding in 1967. Add longtime residents like Charlie Chaplin, Coco Chanel and the immortalized Freddie Mercury (photo), and the Riviera's star power feels timeless.

• Place du Marché, Montreux

Photo: ykaiavu

Wellness

Reset Mode

In a country built for motion, these are the places to slow down, where thermal waters, mountain air and mindful rituals reset the rhythm.

Photo: Agostina Schenone

Still in St. Moritz

Amidst St. Moritz's fast-paced lifestyle, *Mesa Yoga*, the resort's first dedicated yoga studio, offers something the slopes can't: stillness. Inside a sunlit space that feels like an inviting living room, you can explore a range of classes, from gentle restorative sessions to more dynamic flows, alongside guided meditation. A curated bookshop and eco-friendly shop add to the experience beyond the mat, while the friendly, unpretentious atmosphere makes it easy to feel part of the community. By the time you leave, you've found a little calm to carry into the rest of your day.

• Mesa Yoga, Passage au Réduit 15, St. Moritz, mesayoga.studio

Spring Serenity

Therme Vals by award-winning designer Peter Zumthor stands like a monolith in the landscape: raw concrete, Vals quartzite, precise lines. Nothing distracts. Just space, water and echoes. For more than a century, 30-degree thermal water has flowed here from the St. Peter's spring, the only mineral spring in Graubünden. Most pools lie indoors, but from the outdoor pool, the mountains of Vals open up, and at night, the sky fills with stars. Don't miss the night swimming that takes place on select days. Reservations are required.

• 7132 Therme, Poststrasse 560, Vals, 7132.com/en/therme

Soak in Silence

Perched in the Appenzell village of Gonten at 3,000 feet, the five-star *Huus Quell* retreat, part of the *Appenzeller Huus* hotel complex, has been redefining wellness since 2025. Warm materials meet clean lines as guests enjoy sweeping views of the Alpstein. A 24,000-square-foot spa offers everything you need to relax: a rooftop spa with an infinity pool, eight saunas and steam grottos, yoga and meditation rooms, a floating pool and high-tech oxygen treatments. Fireside corners, tea and snacks invite lingering. Best enjoyed with an overnight stay.

• Huus Quell by Appenzeller Huus, Dorfstrasse 40, Gonten, appenzellerhuus.ch

The Brewery Baths

Inside the brick vaults of the former Hürlimann Brewery, the *Aqua Spa*'s mineral-rich thermal water carries you from warm pools into quiet niches. The Roman-Irish spa ritual unfolds in 10 carefully sequenced stages of heat, steam and cooling. The rooftop pool opens onto views across Zurich, which are most atmospheric at sunset or late in the evening. Time slots fill quickly, so booking ahead is wise. For a slower pace, come midweek and pair the baths with a massage. Guests of the *B2 Hotel Zurich* step into the lift and arrive at the spa in moments.

• Hürlimann & Spa, Brandschenkestrasse 150, Zurich, aquaspa.ch

Zen with a View

Above Zermatt, *CERVO Mountain Resort* blends slow luxury with a laid-back cosmopolitan feel, bringing together sustainability, alpine tradition and global inspiration. Boho accents, natural materials and an unobstructed view of the Matterhorn set the tone. At the *Ātman Mountain Spa*, Eastern and Western traditions meet alpine nature. Hotel guests and day visitors alike relax in the onsen, facing the peak and soothing their minds in herbal steam baths and holistic treatments, best followed by a snack on the terrace overlooking the mountains.

• Ātman Mountain Spa, Riedweg 156, Zermatt, cervo.swiss

Captain Your Calm

For a distinctly Swiss take on wellness, skip the spa and take the helm. Wood-fired sauna boats turn the ritual into a simple cycle: fire up, sweat it out, dive into the alpine blue, repeat. Do you prefer hot tubs to saunas? Go with a wood-fired HotTug (photo) that keeps you soaking between cycles, like a slow-cooked escape with killer views. Whether captaining a sauna across Lake Lucerne or steaming through the waters of Lake Brienz, no boating license is required.

• Several locations

Hotels & Lodgings

Swiss Stays

Switzerland's hospitality is as diverse as its landscape, ranging from avant-garde silos to historic postal inns. This curated collection of boutique, design and historic hotels was handpicked for their character and soul. Some earned recognition in the Michelin guide. All are part of Hotels & Lodgings recommended by Switzerland Tourism (switzerland.com/hotels), a national search platform designed to help travelers find hotels that match their specific needs and preferences. Discover the art of the Swiss stay, starting with Boutique & Design Hotels and Lodgings that epitomize personality, creativity and architectural excellence.

Gasthaus Traube, Buchs

Tucked into the small town of Buchs in the St. Gallen Rhine Valley, *Gasthaus Traube* is the kind of discovery you're almost reluctant to share. Part of Marriott Bonvoy's Design Hotels collection, this 14-room guesthouse blends urban polish with alpine calm, making it a refined base in a region that connects Switzerland, Liechtenstein and Austria.

Inside, the mood is intimate and thoughtfully designed without being ostentatious. Natural materials and pared-back interiors create a space that feels contemporary and inviting, resembling more of a private residence than a hotel. The welcome is equally warm: friendly, relaxed and attentive.

What sets Traube apart, however, is its connection to the surrounding area. While Buchs may not be well known, it serves as a gateway to the Bündner Herrschaft wine region, the slopes of Flumserberg and Pizol and lakes such as Walensee and Lake Constance. It's a year-round base for hiking, cycling, skiing or simply slowing down, especially in summer, when the pace softens into a true "coolcation."

Under the guidance of head chef Jonas Grundner, the kitchen offers three distinct dining concepts, ranging from casual fine dining to lighter, vegetable-led dishes. The wine cellar is impressive, featuring one of Switzerland's most extensive champagne selections. Much of what appears on the plate is local, seasonal and made in-house, reflecting a strong connection to regional producers.

Step outside, and a hidden garden offers a final surprise: a calm, green pocket just beyond the town, perfect for enjoying a drink or simply taking a moment to unwind.

• St. Gallerstrasse 7, Buchs, gasthaus-traube.ch

Silo Basel

In a former grain silo once used to store cocoa beans, *Silo Basel* reimagines industrial heritage as one of Switzerland's first true boutique hostels. It blurs the line between hostel and design hotel, offering a thoughtful, architectural stay that is refreshingly unpretentious.

The building's rich history is visible throughout. Raw concrete, exposed structures and generous volumes have been carefully preserved, then softened with warm textures, clean-lined furnishings and a muted, contemporary palette.

Accommodation options range from shared rooms to private ones, all featuring meticulous attention to detail. Even communal spaces are inviting, not just functional, encouraging guests to connect sans the typical hostel chaos. There's a strong sense of flexibility here: Come for a short city break, a creative stopover or a longer holiday.

The location adds to the appeal. Basel's compact center, with its museums, galleries and Rhine-side energy, is within easy reach, while the surrounding neighborhood reflects the city's progressive spirit: international, design-conscious and slightly offbeat.

• Signalstrasse 37, Basel, silobasel.com

Whitepod Original, Les Giettes

High above the Rhône Valley, *Whitepod* offers a stay that is at once futuristic and grounded in nature. Scattered across a mountainside in the heart of Les Giettes (Monthey), Valais, its geodesic pods and cabins sit among the trees, each one positioned to maximize views while minimizing environmental impact.

The concept is simple but effective: low-impact design paired with a high level of comfort. Each space is insulated and energy-efficient, with wood-burning stoves, cozy interiors and large panoramic windows that bring the landscape right inside. It's eco-luxury done with a light touch: thoughtful, immersive and surprisingly comfortable. The outdoors is, unsurprisingly, a main draw. In winter, guests can step straight into snowshoeing, skiing and sledging, with private trails adding to the sense of seclusion. Come summer, the focus shifts to hiking, mountain biking and slow exploration of the surrounding alpine terrain.

Back at base, a central chalet forms the heart of the stay, housing a restaurant that highlights local and seasonal ingredients, alongside spaces to relax after a day outside.

• Route des Cerniers 100 Case postale 681, Les Giettes, whitepod.com

Carlton Hotel St. Moritz

Perched above the lake with sweeping views of the Engadin valley, the *Carlton Hotel St. Moritz* is one of Switzerland's most elegant alpine stays. While its Belle Époque façade speaks to the resort's storied past, the atmosphere inside is far more low-key than traditional luxury might suggest.

Service is impeccable yet personal, and the all-suite setup adds to the hotel's character as well as to its privacy. The accommodations, featuring 60 suites and junior suites, are designed to make the most of the surroundings, with light-filled interiors and uninterrupted views over St. Moritz and the nearby peaks.

A defining feature is also its culinary ambition. The hotel is home to Da Vittorio St. Moritz, awarded two Michelin stars and led by Italian chef Paolo Rota. The Italian dishes are delivered with precision and clarity, balancing tradition with a lighter, modern touch. It's a destination in its own right and a compelling reason to stay.

Beyond the dining room, things move at a slower pace. A spa, sun-drenched terraces and direct access to both winter slopes and summer trails make it easy to shift between activity and stillness. Whether you're here for skiing, hiking or simply the mountain air, everything feels considered.

At its core, the Carlton is a hotel that pairs old-world elegance with a distinctly modern sense of ease, anchored by one of the most exciting dining experiences in the Alps.

• Via Johannes Badrutt 11, St. Moritz, carlton-stmoritz.ch

AlpenGold Hotel, Davos

With its striking, curved façade shimmering above the valley, *AlpenGold Hotel* is hard to miss and even harder to forget. Designed by Munich-based studio Oikios, the building takes inspiration from a pine cone, its layered exterior catching the light as it changes across the mountains.

Inside, the design continues to make a statement. A dramatic wave-like chandelier by Moritz Waldemeyer illuminates the lobby, setting the tone for interiors that combine bold forms with warm, tactile materials. Rooms are generous and light-filled, many with balconies overlooking the landscape around Davos. The watchword here is relaxed luxury, with an emphasis on comfort and subtle detail rather than excess. Dining adds another layer of personality. Alongside refined options, the hotel embraces Swiss tradition with a dedicated Cheese Factory. It's a cozy, convivial space that's all about raclette and fondue, but just as importantly, the atmosphere.

Outside, Davos delivers year-round, from skiing and snowboarding in winter to hiking and biking in the warmer months. Back at the hotel, a spacious spa and sunlit terraces offer a softer counterpoint to the alpine energy.

• Baslerstrasse 9, Davos, alpengoldhotel.com

Le Clay, Puidoux/Lavaux

Opening in late 2026, *Le Clay* marks the debut of the Seiler Constantin collection in the country. Positioned within the UNESCO-listed Lavaux vineyards above Lake Geneva, the hotel has been conceived to immerse guests in one of Switzerland's most cinematic landscapes, where terraced vines cascade toward the water and the Alps rise beyond.

Details remain deliberately understated, but the concept is clearly design-led: architecture and interiors that frame the surroundings, with a focus on light and a restrained yet sleek aesthetic. The overall vibe is chic and laid-back, presenting a modern retreat that lacks the formality of traditional grand hotels.

Life here is shaped by the surroundings. Outside, vineyard paths wind between small wine villages and cellar doors. Lake Geneva lies just below, offering a range of activities from swimming to leisurely boat rides. Lausanne is within easy reach for culture and dining, though many guests will find little reason to leave the calm of the terraces.

• Chemin du Signal 8, Lavaux, leclay.swiss

Park Hyatt Zurich

Park Hyatt Zurich offers a polished, reliable stay with the added benefit of loyalty perks. Part of the Hyatt portfolio, it's a natural choice for travelers looking to earn or redeem points while still seeking design and location.

Set in the heart of Zurich, just steps from Bahnhofstrasse and the lake, the hotel places you within easy reach of the city's shops, galleries and financial district. The building itself leans modern and understated, with clean architectural lines and interiors defined by warm stone, wood and curated art. Rooms are spacious by city standards, with a calm, neutral palette that prioritizes comfort and quiet over statement design. Floor-to-ceiling windows bring in natural light, while thoughtful details, from generous bathrooms to well-considered workspaces, make it equally suited to business and leisure stays.

Dining and wellness round out the offerings. ONYX Bar offers a sleek setting for cocktails, while the restaurant focuses on seasonal cuisine with an international touch. Downstairs, a well-equipped spa and fitness area provide a welcome reset after a day in the city.

• Beethovenstrasse 21, Zurich, hyatt.com/en-US/hotel/switzerland/park-hyatt-zurich

The Omnia, Zermatt

On a rocky ledge above the village of Zermatt, the *Omnia* offers a different perspective on alpine luxury, both literally and stylistically. Reached via a private tunnel and lift, the arrival is oh so cinematic, opening onto a calm, elevated world.

Instead of echoing traditional chalet design, the property leans modern. A mix of wood, stone and glass creates interiors that are effortlessly chic, with plenty of light throughout. The influence of American architect Ali Tayar is evident in the balance between minimalism and comfort, resulting in a mountain lodge reimagined with a contemporary eye. And then, of course, there's the landscape outside. From terraces and many of the rooms, the iconic Matterhorn rises into view, grounding the hotel firmly in its alpine context. It's a backdrop that takes on different moods with the light, from crisp winter mornings to softer summer evenings.

Days here might begin with skiing or hiking directly from the village, followed by time in the spa—an indoor-outdoor space carved into the rock—or a long, relaxed dinner that draws on seasonal ingredients with a modern European touch. If you're after a sleek retreat that manages to be deeply connected to the mountains around it, this is your place.

• Auf dem Fels 3920, Zermatt, the-omnia.com

Swiss Historic Hotels and Lodgings: From here, we shift from boutique and design hotels to stays shaped by history and tradition.

Hotel Stern und Post, Amsteg

Our historic hotel recommendations begin along the Gotthard Route, a centuries-old alpine crossing, with *Hotel Stern und Post.* Set in the small village of Amsteg in the heart of the Gotthard region, this long-standing inn blends heritage and modern comfort in a way that is both grounded and refreshingly current.

Back in 1788, the property was one of Switzerland's first post offices, welcoming travelers crossing the Alps, among them figures such as Johann Wolfgang von Goethe and Hans Christian Andersen. That sense of history is still present today, woven into the building's thick walls, timber details and enduring role as a place of rest along an important route.

Interiors have been thoughtfully updated, balancing tradition with a lighter, contemporary feel. The rooms follow suit: simple and warm, designed less for show and more for genuine comfort. Food, too, is integral in the hotel's character. The restaurant focuses on regional cuisine driven by seasonality and local produce, reflecting the spirit of the surrounding valley.

With hiking trails beginning just beyond the doorstep and the wider Gotthard region offering mountain passes, historic routes and alpine landscapes, the setting encourages leisurely exploration.

• Gotthardstrasse 88, Amsteg, stern-post.ch

Post Hotel Löwe, Mulegns

In the tiny village of Mulegns, where the Julier Pass road winds through dramatic mountain scenery, the *Post Hotel Löwe* stands as a striking example of heritage brought back to life. The Origen Cultural Foundation has carefully restored this historic inn, once a vital stop for travelers crossing the Alps, preserving its past while giving it renewed purpose.

Dating back to the 19th century, the building retains its original character, from frescoed walls and period details to the sense of scale typical of grand alpine coaching inns. Yet the restoration avoids turning it into a museum piece. Instead, it remains welcoming, with a focus on authenticity over polish. Rooms are simple and intentionally unshowy, allowing the architecture and history to do most of the talking. They make for an accommodation that genuinely reflects the traditions of the region.

The hotel is closely tied to Origen's cultural program, meaning your stay may coincide with performances, installations or events that bring contemporary creativity into dialogue with the historic setting. Outside, the surrounding landscape offers hiking routes, mountain passes and a sense of remoteness that's increasingly rare. If you value atmosphere and history, don't miss it.

• Veia Gelgia 89, Mulegns, origen.ch/hotels

Château Salavaux

In the gentle countryside of the Three Lakes Region, *Château Salavaux* offers an inviting take on the château stay. Surrounded by vineyards and just a short distance from Lake Murten, this 16th-century estate blends historic character with a relaxed, modern-day feel.

The setting is idyllic. Rolling vines, soft light and open landscapes frame the scene, with the lake adding a subtle Mediterranean touch in the warmer months. It's a place made for slowing your pace and trading your everyday routine for long walks, unhurried afternoons and evenings that stretch out over a very good dinner. Inside, the design blends heritage with simplicity. Original architectural details sit alongside modern touches, creating spaces that are warm and informal. Rooms are individually styled, but all share the same easygoing comfort.

Food and wine are naturally central to the experience. The surrounding region is known for its vineyards, and the château embraces that connection, with local produce and regional wines taking center stage.

• Route de Villars-le-Grand 16, Salavaux, chateausalavaux.ch

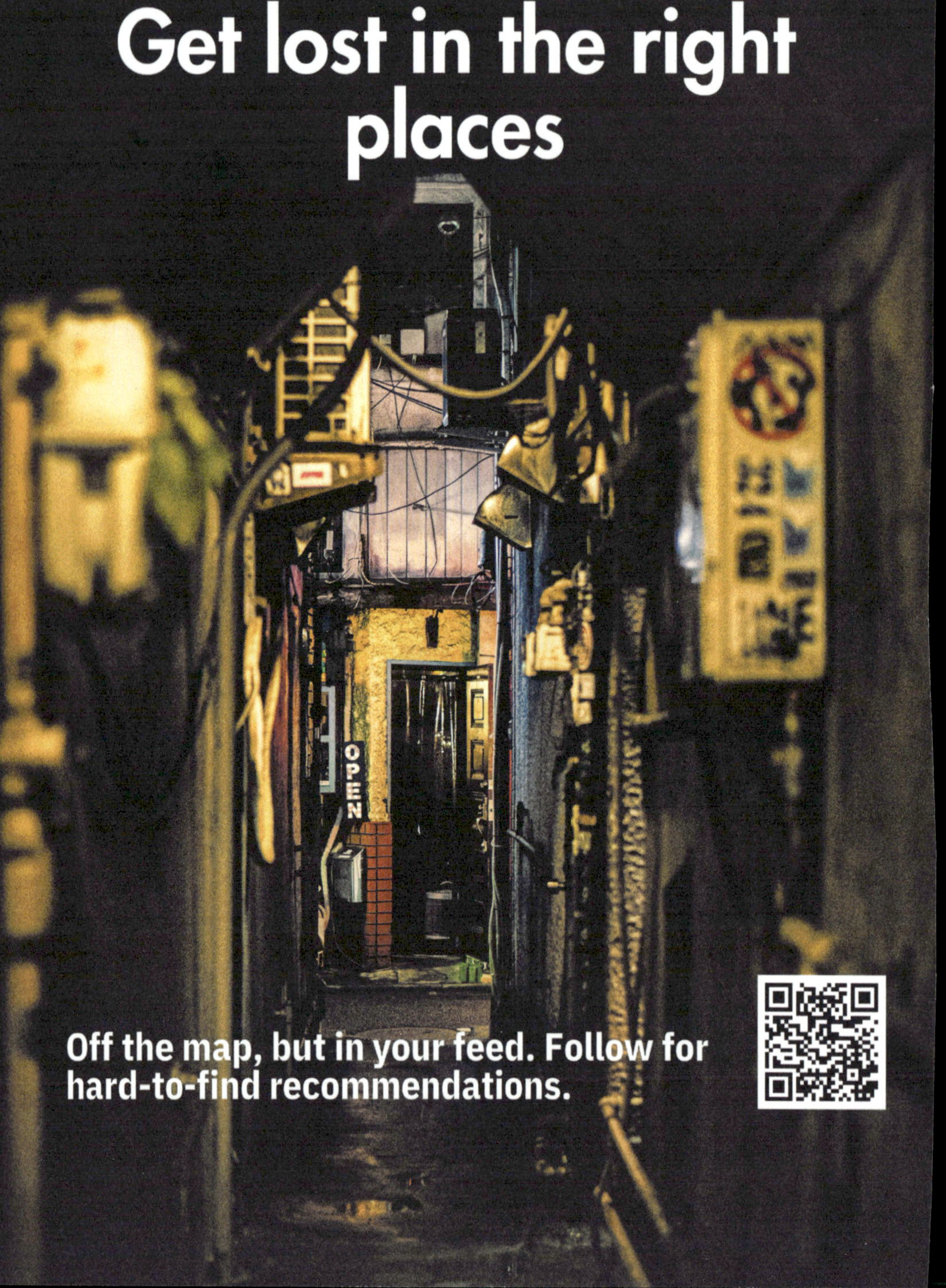

Get lost in the right places

Off the map, but in your feed. Follow for hard-to-find recommendations.